The Summer of 2013

I Remember Hartford

By

William "Rab" Smith

In the Beginning

I was born the 1st child of Ben and Pearl Woods Smith on Wednesday, February 10, 1926. My mother used to call me "Willie Robert" because my full name is William Robert Smith.

When I was born, my parents lived at 158-160 Wooster Street. We were on the 1st floor at 160, when I was little, and then later on, we moved to the 2nd floor which was 158. I cannot remember all of my brothers and sisters living at 160 but I do remember, everyone including all of my brothers and sisters, living at 158. The names and year of birth of the children in my family in order were; William (that's me 1926), Thelma (1928), Ben (1930), Charlie (1931) and Barbara (1934).

My father and mother probably met at Mount Calvary Church which stood on Charter Oak Avenue, at the time. The building is still there, on Charter Oak Avenue but the Mount Calvary Congregation moved to Mahl Avenue in the early 1950's.

My parents married in 1925. My maternal grandparents were from Georgia but they moved here to Hartford before I was born. Their names were Jack and Lizzie Woods. Lizzie's maiden name was Bronnan. Jack was a founding member of Mount Calvary Baptist Church and Lizzie was a member of the first Muslim Mosque here in the City of Hartford. It was known as the Moorish American Science Temple.

This is a photograph of my Father, Mother and me in 1926.
I was 1 year old.

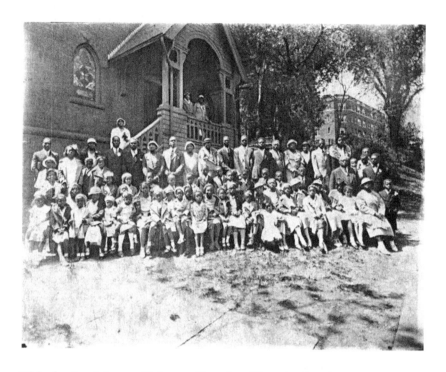

This is the Mount Calvary Baptist Church Sunday school circa 1933. I remember my family taking the trolley to church when we lived on Wooster Street; boy did that trolley ride make me sick. That's my cousin Gladys (second row from the front, 4th from the left) and the next child (second row 5th from the left) is me.

Although the 1900 records indicate that my mother was living in Militia District 978, Webster, Georgia at the time, my mother came out of Richland, Georgia which was not far from Americus, Georgia. My Grandparents on my Mother's side were Jack and Eliza Woods. Jack was born during the Civil War in 1863. Since this was soon after the signing of the Emancipation Proclamation, he was one of the first blacks born free in the south. Eliza's formal name was Mary Elizabeth Wood. So both my grandmothers had basically the same name, Liza for my Father's Mother and Lizzie for my mother's mother. My maternal Grandmother had 2 sisters (my great aunts) who I never knew, Maggie Holly and Katie Wright. She also had a brother I never knew (my Great Uncle) named Richard Cuff. They never came to Hartford.

My mother's parents actually came up to Hartford around 1916 and lived. I don't know where they lived when they first got to Hartford but when I was 4, they were living at 53 Sanford Street. That's where they lived when my grandfather, Jack Woods, died. I remember him very well. The thing that I remember most was he always had black Smith Brothers, or Ludens cough drops which he would buy for five cents a box. I could always get one of those cough drops from him. I didn't like the Ludens because they were so strong. The Smith Brothers were strong too because they were like licorice, black, and the Ludens were tan and they had a mediciny taste like Vicks. I also remember being with him when the train came by on Windsor Street. Whenever he would hear the train whistle blow he would take out his watch and say "five minutes slow." He wasn't talking about his watch he was talking about the train. His watch was never wrong; trust me, never as far as he was concerned! I think he worked on the railroad at one time. "He was a real mover and a shaker". He had his own fish market, which was at 82 Bellevue Street. I vaguely remember my Mother bringing me into his store. He was the Chairman of the Deacon Board of Mount Calvary Baptist Church. He was also a Charter member and was serving as the Treasurer of that church when he died in September of 1930. The day he died, he came by the house on Wooster Street in a car. People had taken him to see some Indian doctor, because he had asthma or something; he used to sleep mostly sitting up in a chair. When he would lay down he couldn't get his breath. I think he died on his back porch sitting in his chair on Sanford Street.

Jack's Wife was named Eliza, and her maiden name was Bronnan according to my parents' marriage certificate. We used to call her "Ma Woods" because she didn't like to be called Grandma. My Cousin Gladys called her Ma because she raised Gladys after Gladys' mother died. Gladys' mother died when she was very young. Gladys' mother was married to Jack Woods Junior, who was my Uncle. I don't remember Gladys' mother's first name but her maiden name was Haywood. I had two first cousins named Walter and Emily McBride. Their mother Fannie was my mother's sister. Walter and Emily McBride called her grandma; they were the only ones who got away with it.

My mother used to say that her mother had some Indian in her, and judging from the photos that I saw of her she looked like she might have. However, based upon the reading that I have done, the majority of the people breeding with African American's were not Indian, they were white. Mostly Irish indentured servants. Due to the large numbers that were created by these slaves and indentured servants breeding, the owners used to have to tell the white servants "you're better than they are" because you're white". That prevented them from uniting and making things dangerous for the masters. My mother knew Ma Woods' father (my great grandfather) but I never heard her say anything about her maternal grandmother (my great grandmother).

For a while, my mother's maternal grandfather, (Peter Bronner) actually stayed with my mother, her parents and her brothers, Walter, Jack, and Fred. Her brother Ulysses, and her brother Ester and her sisters Fannie and Dolly were not born yet. When I was a kid, my mother used to tell me about her maternal grandfather, Peter Bronner. I think he was the one whose wife had been sold off. Her name was Sarah Cuff. I'm not sure if they were actually married but he had permission to go and see her at night. He would have to travel twenty miles and get back by the next morning.

Now, I know that it is possible to walk twenty miles in one day, but to do that and come back and work as a field hand or whatever. She used to also tell me how when she was a child, her maternal grandfather (that would be Lizzie Bronnan-Woods Father), would walk around with his cane during the rain. Wherever he walked, his cane would stick holes in the ground. Long after his death, you could still see the holes where he had walked. I believe he was the one who was once a slave and when his slave master went away to fight in the Civil War, he gave my great grandfather all his silver and gold money. My great grandfather hid the money, buried it I guess, and when his slave master came back my great grandfather gave the money back to him.

Here's my grandmother Mary Elizabeth Bronner-Woods (I called her "Ma Woods") back in Webster County Georgia around 1896. The children are from left to right: my uncle Walter, my uncle Jack (in the dress), my mother Pearl, and in Ma Woods' arms is Fred. Ulysses, Fannie, Esther (Esther was a boy) and Dolly were not born yet. Esther's nickname was Dude. He was born in 1904 and was 23 years old when he drowned in the Connecticut River.

My mother's paternal grandfather was named Andrew Wood. He was born in 1810 and lived to be at least 98 years old. He was Jack Woods' father.

I remember when my maternal grandmother, Mary Elizabeth Woods, turned 65. It was in the year 1935 which was the year when social security came out. People who were 65 and over were grandfathered into the system. Therefore, they got social security payments of about 8 or 10 dollars a month. Of course, you could rent a house for 15. Our apartment on Wooster Street cost 15 dollars a month. My Grandmother died while I was in the service in 1945. So she lived to be 75 years old. Ma Woods (Mary Elizabeth) died while she was in Woodstock, Connecticut, in 1945. I was in Hawaii serving in the Navy.

My uncle Jack, who once had a restaurant on Canton Street, had a daughter by the name of Gladys Woods. Gladys' mother died when she was very young so Gladys lived with my grandparents. I remember Gladys; Gladys married a guy by the name of Walter Lowe. Gladys died in childbirth at the age of about 16 at the old Municipal Hospital at 2 Holcomb Street. Her funeral was at Johnson's funeral home on Pavilion

Street. The approximate year of this occurrence was 1937.

On my mother's father's side of the family (the Woods side) were the Pertillar's. My mother's father (Jack Woods) and a man named Richard Countryman were first cousins. My maternal grandparents, Lizzie and Jack Woods wrote to Ed Countryman and told him to come to Connecticut. Ed came to Hartford in July of 1917 with his brother Baurel. One week later, Ed sent for his father, Richard Countryman. He in turn, sent for his wife, Julia Ward Countryman and his daughter, Clara. They all stayed with my grandparents Lizzie and Jack Woods until they found an apartment on Canton Street. Baurel and Clara attended Arsenal School when they moved here so they must have been children at the time.

Richard Countryman was the father of several sons and daughters, one of which was Clara Countryman who married Charlie Pertillar. That would have made Richard Countryman my mother's second cousin and Richard's daughters and sons would be my mother's third cousins. Charlie Pertillar was the first person I ever knew who had a telephone. This was sometime in the mid 1930's. He lived on Wooster Street, between Pavilion and Canton Street. He was a trucker or someone who transported things with his truck and he needed a telephone so people could call him to do work.

When I was a kid, Grandma Woods used to make what she called "preservatives" in Hellman's Mayonnaise jars. After she made them, she would give me one that I could have for my very own. It was a condensed fruit, the best stuff in the world. My mother and my grandmother could cook and can, we never ran out of food. Didn't have any money at all but we always had food. Everybody loved to come to our house because you could always eat. Even during the depression we had food. It was during that time men that we used to call "tramps" would come to the back door and ask for food.

My mother never turned anybody away; she would give them some bread or something. We didn't have bacon but we had what they called "Streak of Lean Salt Pork". My mother would fry that hard. She also had biscuits that I didn't like because they were too doughy in the middle. I would squash them down and put jelly or salt pork in the middle. Well, my mother would always give them something. Everybody who ever came to that door got something to eat. One day, I asked her, "Ma why are you always giving our food away", and one day she told me; "you don't know when Jesus is coming or how He is coming. You don't know what He looks like because you haven't seen Him." That would shut me up because I could never answer that, in my mind even. That's the way she was.

My grandmother (Ma Woods) actually lived with my family when I was in the Navy. She had gotten too old to take care of herself but because she joined the Moorish American Temple in the late 1930's she did spend time at a Moorish Science Temple commune in Woodstock Connecticut. The Moorish Americans were Muslims founded in 1921 by Nobel Drew Ali. The person who introduced it here in Hartford was known as the Grand Sheik by the name of E. Turner- El. Because the names of black people were taken from slave masters, Muslims in the 30's added "El" or "Bey" to separate them from their slave names. How it was determined who became El's and who became Bey's, I don't know. I don't know anybody today by the name of El but I do know people by the name of Bey. My Grandmother Lizzie was an El. The Woodstock commune was almost in Rhode Island.

I was in California in April, when President Franklin D. Roosevelt died, so my grandmother, Lizzie Woods must have died in May of 1945. The war in Europe ended in April or May of '45. So I must have gone to Hawaii in May. That's when she passed away while she was living at the commune, May 13, 1945 at the age of 76. I could not get back for the funeral because I was so far away but my cousin Walter was stationed in Virginia, at the time, so he came home for the funeral. When she died she left behind two sisters, Mrs. Maggie Holly and Mrs. Katie Wright, of Dawson, Georgia. I also had an aunt by the name of Delphee or Delphi who lived in Atlanta, Georgia. She lived on Peach Tree Street. Grandma Woods also had a brother named Richard Cuff of Dawson. I never knew about her sisters or her brother. Her sons Walter, Jack (who was named after his father), Ulysses, and Fred, lived on with the exception of the one they called "Dude" who drowned in the Connecticut River. Dude's real name was Ester Woods. He died July 23, 1926, just a little more than 5 months after I was born. He was just 23 years old when he drowned after falling off the Willimantic Bridge (the old train trestle just north of the Bulkeley Bridge). I don't know if he fell off that bridge, or if someone pushed him, or what happened. Ma Woods also left behind the following daughters; my mother Pearl, and my aunts; Fannie and Dolly.

My Uncle Walter also lived at 53 Sanford Street but he had his own apartment because he was married. He lived up on the third floor and my grandmother lived on the first floor. Jack didn't live there but his daughter, Gladys did. My grandmother raised her when Gladys' mother died. Ulysses lived somewhere else. Fred lived there on and off most of the time. Those four uncles (Walter, Jack, Ulysses and Fred), I remember well. However, they didn't live long. Fred was my favorite uncle. He was a barber and was fond of a drink now and then. Some people wouldn't let him cut their hair unless he was drunk. Out of all my uncles, Fred lived the longest even though he had tuberculosis. He would stay with us on Garden Street when he had furloughs but most of the time he was at Cedar Crest Hospital in Newington, CT. That's where he died.

My Maternal Grandmother, Lizzie Woods

My Maternal Grandfather, Jack Woods

My Aunt, Fannie

Here's my Aunt Fannie and my Cousins Walter and Emily. Her husband's name was "Rojer" (pronounced row-jer) so she was also known as Mrs. R. G. McBride.

My Uncle, Fred Woods. He was my favorite Uncle. I believe this is the uncle that was in Ma Woods' arms in the photo on page 12.

Here's my Uncle Jack Woods Jr.

The History of Big Ben

My father, Benjamin Smith, was born October 4th, 1892 in Americus, Georgia to Eliza and Mark Smith. Eliza's maiden name was Bivens. His parents (my paternal grandparents) never came to Hartford. After my grandfather, Mark, passed away, my father's parents' house burned down. I thought this would mean that my grandmother Eliza would move here to Hartford, but instead, my father took the train down there and built the house back up. This happened around 1936, when I was about 10 or 11 years old. How he did that I don't know because that was during the heart of the depression. His older brother, Robert Smith, did come up to Hartford for a little while, didn't like it and went back to Georgia. That's where he stayed until he died. My father's mother had 2 children by her first husband, including my father and his brother, Robert. Through a second marriage, his mother then had Louise, Jordan, and a set of twins, William was one of the twins and the other one died during childbirth. My father had a cousin named Mae Willie who moved from Georgia to Detroit. He had another cousin, Mary Elizabeth, who lived with her husband, Sam King, on Wooster Street when we did.

There were no kids of my age on my father's side of the family up here. They were all down south. My Aunt Louise and my Uncle Jordan didn't have any kids. Louise was born March 21, 1900, the first day of spring that year, she was known to all family members as "Nanny" and she lived in the Hartford area until 1993. She lived to be 92 years old. My father's older brother, Robert, had several kids who my Aunt Louise used to keep in touch with and later on my sister, Thelma, stayed in touch with. I never had any correspondence with them and I never went down south until 1945 when I was in the Navy down in Virginia. I never went to Georgia until the early 1970's when I went to an Elks convention in New Orleans and I stopped in Atlanta on the way back. I never went down to Americus (where my Father was born) until long after my daughter, Finitia, was down there. I drove down there with my wife, Agnes, and my 2 granddaughters, Nickia Miller and Meisha Armstrong, but I didn't know anybody down there.

My father was not the kind of man to get angry enough to hit us kids. Because of the way he would grab us when he got mad, we thought he would kill us, but he never did. My mother was the killer. My Father never forgot how bad things were in the Jim Crow south. He would tell me stories that made me vow never to go down there. That's the reason why I never met my paternal grandmother. She wanted to come to Hartford but her responsibilities as a farm owner prevented her from doing so. She had to milk the cows, feed the chickens, and take care of crops that were planted. I didn't find out until I was grown that a woman named Henrietta Welch who lived on Mahl Avenue also had family that lived where my father's parents lived in Americus, Georgia. Welch was her married name because she married William Welch who was a World War 2 veteran. I don't know what her family name was. Apparently, my father's parents used to raise a pig for Mrs. Welch's family. Her family would pay for the feed and other expenses of caring for the pig. This was an annual thing. Once the pig was big enough it would be slaughtered and Mrs. Welch's family would get the meat.

    My grandmother had a smoke house where the meat was cured and then it would be salted for preservation. My grandmother would actually send some of the meat from Georgia to Hartford by rail and personnel from a company named Railway Express would deliver the meat to various houses by truck. The meat would arrive at our house wrapped in cheesecloth. We did not have refrigerators back then but we had an icebox during the summer time. We would hang the meat up in the pantry. Although the meat would turn green around the edges, you could cut it into slab bacon and wash it off. Because of all the salt, the meat would not spoil. However, if you left it next to a lot of heat, it could get rancid otherwise it would last a half a year.

In those days, it was common for people to plant things, harvest it and preserve it over the winter. My father kept things in the basement. I remember helping him wrap apples in newspaper and place potatoes in sand. If they rotted they would rot individually, and not ruin the other fruits and vegetables. My mother would take tomatoes and can them. My father would pick wild blue berries and she would also can those. At that time, Connecticut was full of wild blueberries. If you had permission from the land owners, you could pick them. Connecticut was an agricultural state. You could find things like these and tobacco in great abundance. I used to love pickled watermelon rind. If we had a watermelon with a thick rind, my mother would make pickles out of it. It had a sour sweet taste like it was made with vinegar, cloves, and sugar. They were good, especially to eat with greens or whatever. You sliced it up. I used to love that stuff. I wish I knew how to do it.

When I was a kid you could take your wagon to one of the slaughter houses on Donald Street. If they had just slaughtered a cow or a pig you could get some of the tripe (stomach) and intestines (chitterlings). Then you could bring it home in your wagon to eat. I wouldn't eat it back then. At first, this was free until people started having fights in the line. Back then, only black people would eat this that I knew of. Then, one of the Chicago packing houses started putting chitterlings in buckets with ice. They would then ship it by rail and sell it. In those days, you could buy a ten pound bucket for four dollars.

This is my mother, Pearl Woods, before she and my father were married. They were married in 1925.

Here's my father Ben Smith during World War One. He left the service in 1919.

Hard Times Hit Hartford

1929 was the year that the great depression hit the United States of America. However, the truly negative effects were not felt in my household until 1930. That was the year that my father lost his job. He had been working at The Hartford Lumber Company, on Albany Avenue. It's still there at the same location. Usually, he worked there as a yard person and on some nights he would work additional hours as the night watchman. I can still remember the revolver he carried when he came home between shifts. It was a great big 38' caliber revolver. Or, at least, it looked big to me at the time. When you are little, everything looks big. On some days my mother and I would walk from our home on Wooster Street to the Keney Clock Tower to have lunch. In those days the park surrounding the Tower, was only reserved for women, and children less than six years of age. It was then that my father would leave the lumber yard, come across Albany Avenue and Main Street while we were in the Keney Clock Tower Park. When we saw him coming we would leave the park and walk with him home to Wooster Street. After we had lunch he would walk back to the lumber company by himself. This is one of the things that I remember clearly when I was just four and a half years old. He lost that job when the Great Depression hit because nobody was building houses. He didn't go back to work until President Franklin Delano Roosevelt became President of the United States. It was through a program that F.D.R. created called the W.P.A. that my Father went back to work. I remember my Father working on Brainerd Field and the dike.

During the war, which started in 1941, he worked in factories, initially, in New Britain and eventually in Plainville. That's where he worked until he retired. His Sister, my Aunt Nanny, worked for a person by the name of Soby who was a part owner of a factory. The Soby family lived on Terry Road, in Hartford at one time. Then they moved to a mansion that the family built on Soby Drive in West Hartford. I was told that that building cost $25,000.00. I've been in that house. I think it has twenty or twenty five rooms in it. I used to play with the son of the Soby family by the name of Tommy and I got some of his hand me down toys. I remember being there in the early 1930's and wanting a particular toy and he wouldn't give it to me. At one time Nanny worked for a family by the name of Burke who lived in Rockville. Can you imagine getting up and getting on a trolley or a bus and going to work in

Rockville every day? When she bought her house on Taft Avenue in Bloomfield, she borrowed the money from a person she worked for by the name of Mr. Holman from Manchester. She paid him on a regular basis until one day he simply forgave the note.

Here is my aunt Nanny. Her name was Louise Edwards. This photo was taken on March 22, 1980. She was 80 years old. She lived until 1993.

I can vividly remember being in the kindergarten in 1931, walking down Wooster Street and coming home for lunch. I went half days, I started out in afternoon kindergarten and ended going to school in the morning. Later on, as I was going through the various grades, I can remember wanting to go from school to Shiloh Baptist Church on Albany Avenue to eat lunch. Back then, you could get a full meal for a nickel. You would get lunch, milk, and desert. But I had to go home. My mother would have lunch at home because my mother was a stay at home housewife.

At Shiloh, Reverend Moody was the Pastor. Reverend King Hayes followed him. Shiloh has been in the same location for all of my life. Right now, Reverend Powell is conducting services there. He started out at Mount Calvary. I was at his first sermon. We were renovating upstairs and his sermon was given downstairs. It was packed. He was ordained under this pastor we've got now, by the name of Richard Nash. Reverend Powell's main Church is Antioch on Nelson Street. Nice person, Jeff. Good demeanor.

My Introduction to the Elks and the Masons

Originally, there was one Elks Lodge in Hartford, and then there became two. The original Elks lodge was named Nutmeg Lodge number 67. It was located on Morgan Street. That's the one that my father and one of his friends named Elbert Bland, joined in 1917 just before he went into the Army during WW1. He obtained the rank of Corporal.

The Elks were founded in Hartford as Nutmeg number 67 in 1905; it actually went from one lodge to two lodges in the early 1930's. Nutmeg became "New Nutmeg" and another lodge was formed under the name of "Charter Oak Lodge number 67". So they both kept the number 67 because the numbers told when they were founded. The Grand Exalted Ruler approved of these two lodges having the same number. The lower the number the closer a lodge came to the original founding date. Some numbers became defunct, like the number 1. That lodge was formed in Cincinnati, Ohio and it is no longer used. I decided that I wanted to become an Elk immediately after I was sworn into the Navy in New Haven and I was on my way to Chicago, to

Great Lakes for boot camp. A whole bunch of people got on the train with all of these bags of chicken and ham and booze. By the time we got to Grand Central Station in New York there were people who had gotten on the train at every stop. They were all the same, very jovial people. I then turned to Mansfield Tilly and told him "man I'm joining that organization as soon as I get out of here." He said "stay away from that organization, you don't need that." I said "oh yeah, don't nobody have more fun than these people." I thought it was the most wonderful thing in the world. Prior to that time I had heard of Elks. In fact, before I was old enough to go inside, when I was about sixteen and seventeen, during the summer, I used to go down to Canton Street and stand outside the back of the Elks Club building and listen to the music that was coming from inside. Since the back of the building was right next to the bandstand, I could hear everything.

When I was a member of Charter Oak Lodge, we relocated to Blue Hills Avenue from 59 Canton Street, to an old First National Supermarket. On Canton Street, we occupied all of the first floor and half of the second floor. It was a tenement until the last residents moved out, then, sometime in the 1950's, we rented it to the forerunner of our Masonic lodge, Tuscan. At the time I believe they were known as "International" a clandestine lodge. As a matter of fact, one of the members of our Elks Club gave me hell for renting to them. He asked me "didn't you know that those guys are clandestine?" I told him I didn't know what they were. They told me that they had a Masonic Lodge, they needed some place to meet, and they wanted to rent the space. I told them that we were not financially able to renovate the space. They told me that they would take care of it and they did. In fact, they took better care of the place than any tenant we had in the last twenty years. Some of the tenants we had wouldn't even pay their rent. These men paid their rent and fixed the place up so well that their lodge looked better than ours. They had workmen in their lodge that did that work. Subsequently, in 1961, they healed their lodge and became Tuscan number 17.

Some of their members consisted of Lewis Myrick, Ben Monroe, and Clifton Green (who used to have the beauty supply business on Nelson Street where Antioch Baptist Church is now). Our Grand Master Charles Robinson bought that barber shop after it moved from Garden Street to Westland Street and that's where it is now. That Lodge became defunct because we could not amortize the mortgage. We maintained the Lodge but we held our meetings on Bellevue Street. As time progressed and we didn't have plans to get another building we decided to merge again. That's when the lodge currently on Bellevue Street became New Nutmeg Charter Oak Lodge number 67. The building on Bellevue Street used to be a house. It became an Elks Lodge in the 1930's.

When I was a little kid, right after the split, I believe they were around the corner on Pavilion Street but I'm not sure about hat. I can vaguely remember those guys sitting out in front of the building on Pavilion Street when I was a kid. The building in the back, behind the Bellevue Street building, was designed by Connie Nappier. Manny Gomes was your late uncle on your mother's side. He was married to your Aunt Gida. He was an Elk and his wake and funeral were in the building in the back, upstairs where we have our lodge meetings. I can distinctly remember him saying that he was going to have his funeral there but I always thought he was kidding. What I didn't know was that he had actually put it in his will. That's where he had it. The building on Bellevue Street used to be used to hold Christmas parties for kids, repasts, weddings, baby showers, and birthday parties for people in the neighborhood. In 1964, when I became District Deputy, we had two lodges. At the lodge on Bellevue Street there was an older member of the lodge named Mr. Bland. Mr. Bland used to visit our house on Wooster Street practically every day when I was a kid. One day he told me that he and my father joined the Elks way back in 1918 when there was just one lodge on Morgan Street. Prior to that day (in 1964) I didn't even know that my father was even a member. When the Great Depression hit and my father had us children, he didn't affiliate because he had lost his job and couldn't afford it.

I also remember seeing his fez for the Knights of Pythias, which is another organization entirely, and was founded in 1848 in Mississippi. This is an organization that was founded as a burial society and it became a fraternal order. They used to meet at the Elks building on Bellevue Street. This organization is no longer active in Hartford because all of the members died out. The only person I know who is still living is Frank Richardson. Frank's wife Rachael just turned 100 years old. I was asked to serve as the keynote speaker at their national event in New Britain. The name of my speech was "Where do we go from here?" To research the speech I had to call the library of Congress and get information from a book that was written on the organization. There were only 3 places in the world that had the publication I needed to conduct my research;

Rutgers University in New Jersey, the Schaumburg Institute of Black and Hispanic Studies in New York, and the Library of Congress. While I was there trying to review my speech, a guy came to the door and asked me "is this where they are going to have the affair for the Knights of Pythias?" I said, "yeah, you are in the right place."

He then asked me "I'm staying right across the street, I've been on the road for two weeks and I've been eating a lot of rubber chicken. Do you think I have enough time to go across the street to get something to eat?" I told him that there was going to be food at this banquet and it would not be rubbery because these ladies know how to cook. As I got closer to him his face began to look familiar. It was Benjamin Hooks! That floored me because he was someone who I always idolized. He had just been elected the Grand Chancellor of the Knights of Pythias. He was incredible. He was a lawyer, a Baptist Minister and became President of the National NAACP. When I completed my speech I came to realize that no one in the organization knew about the book I used to conduct the research. Not even the Grand Chancellor. I told them that they had the right to get copies of the book because it belonged to them. They were the only people in the world who had that right.

Here I am shaking hands with Benjamin Hooks later on that evening at the Pride of Connecticut, Elks Lodge. The other men are from left to right; the Vice Chancellor of the Knights of Pythias (name unknown) and the Chief of the New Britain Police Department, Clifford Willis (representing the Mayor of New Britain).

Many years later I spoke with a man named Jerome Lynch who was about seven or eight years older than me. He told me that he knew my father because my father was a Mason. My father used to go over to Jerome's house at night when Jerome's father was dying. My father did this every night until Jerome's father passed away. My father would do this and then get dressed in the morning and go to work. Now, that's three organizations that my father belonged to.

This Was My Neighborhood

*During WWII, Hartford had around 175,000 people living in it. It now has 120,000…*William "Rab" Smith

In any event, my childhood was very mundane. Although I was born and raised in Hartford, it felt like I lived out of town. I say this because Windsor Avenue (which was that portion of "Main Street" north of Albany Avenue) used to start at "the Tunnel". The original "tunnel" is where the train traveled underground in Hartford and that takes place where Main and Albany Avenue intersect. Anything north of "the Tunnel" was thought of as out of town when I was a kid. Hartford seemed to start at Capen Street and extended south. Because back in my day communities were self-sustaining, there were many businesses in my neighborhood. So, the layout of my neighborhood consisted of the following:

Main Street

There was a store at the corner of Main and Capen Street named the "Windsor Avenue Pharmacy". Even though the name of the street changed from Windsor Avenue to Main Street in the late 1920's, the name of the Pharmacy remained the same until at least the late 30's. Eventually, Windsor Avenue was named Main Street past Capen Street and went all the way into Windsor. Up until the late 1930's, the place once known as "Main Tower", next to U-Haul, was a restaurant known as "Otto's. It was a "road house" and it was like out of town. The car dealership across the street from Otto's was once known as "On the Hill but On the Level" and it's been there forever. L.B. Barnes' Funeral Parlor was also on Main Street north of Suffield Street now known as Battles Street. It was north of where Mount Olive Church now stands. Actually the funeral home stood where part of the parking lot now is. The owners of this establishment have 2 children now living in the area, a son and a daughter. If you looked south on Main Street, from the corner of Suffield Street (now known as Battles Street) there stood the following businesses: Fitchman's grocery store was on the corner of Main and Suffield Streets, next was Charlie Garsoon's Chinese Laundry. Charlie lived in the back. Next to him was an Italian Barber Shop. At one time, the Independent Social Center controlled the corners of Main, Suffield and Wooster Streets. Next to the barber shop was the Independent Social Center, and then came the Lincoln Dairy ice cream shop. They had the best ice cream in the world. I can honestly say that I tried every flavor they sold but nothing topped a super banana split they had called "the Nightmare". It was called that because you would have a nightmare if you ate one. Some of the people that worked there were two women named Florence and Gerry, a guy named Holmes, and later on a guy named Alphonso Wright. Even my brother-in-Law Charlie Daniels worked there.

The Lincoln Dairy once stood next door to where A.M.E. Zion's administrative office building now stands. In the late 1940's, Ella Brown, Hartford's first black female police officer lived in the apartment above Lincoln Dairy. Another ice cream shop that everyone remembers is Helen's Double Dip which was south of the Daly Theatre. If you started at the Tunnel and went south, you would run into the Daly Theatre, two or three doors south of the Daly Theatre was Helens' Double Dip ice cream shop. Helen was known for her "lemon ice". There, you could get two dips of ice cream for a dime. However, the scoops were not as big and the ice cream was not as good as the Lincoln Dairy. That was the best ice cream in the world. They even had orange pineapple, coconut pineapple and black cherry. After that was a building that still stands which was also occupied by the Independent Social Center. Next to that, was a 6 family apartment building, which is still there. Then came the Windsor Avenue Congregational Church, now known as Faith Congregational Church. Next came the S and M (Sidney and Mary) Johnson's Funeral Parlor, and then there were 2 multiple family apartment buildings. There was a package store, a barber shop and then a drug store. At the very corner was "Pavilion Drug" which had a soda fountain, a candy counter and over the counter medicine. Next came Pavilion Street.

There was a Benzoline gas station on the southeast corner of Main and Pavilion Street. Blacks have owned that station since about 1946. Some of the men who owned it were John Scott, and Philmore Troutman. After them, George Ware and then Tom Parish owned it. That area is now officially known as "Tom Parish corner". It was named after Tom Parish because of his extensive community involvement. John Scott was a World War II veteran and he married a relative of Phil's.

After you left the corner of Main and Pavilion Streets and walked south, there were two 6 tenement houses, and the Atlantic Gas Station on the same side of the street. Then there were the widow's homes, which still stand today. Next to them was the Arsenal School which stood at 1800 Main Street. That's where everyone learned to swim from a gym teacher named "Smiler" Livingston. He taught everyone but me. I learned how in the Navy. Further down Main Street, across the street from Engine Company 2's firehouse, there was a hotel named "Highland Court". Interstate busses used to bring guest to and from there. At one time Main Street was Route 5 and it was one of the stops on that route. They had businesses on the bottom floor. They also had a Turkish bath inside. I know one guy who got some kind of infection from that. In later years, (sometime in the 1950's or early 60's) George Swan bought it and Sonny Fredrick had a store there at one time.

There was also a gas station on the corner of Capen and Main Street and one next to where the driveway of where the American Legion now stands. The owner of the station, at the corner of Main and Capen, got busted for messing around with rationing coupons during the WWII. Tom Jenkins' father and Ed Smith's father wound up owning the station where the American Legion now stands at one point and time.

Right next to the American Legion on Main Street was an A&P grocery store. It was where Star Hardware is now. At one time A&P was one of the largest chain grocery stores in the country. A&P stood for the great Atlantic and Pacific Tea Company.

Pavilion Street

Pavilion Street used to be just 2 blocks long. It went from Main to Wooster and then Wooster to Bellevue Street. On the south east corner of Wooster and Pavilion Street I believe there was an apartment building. After that there were more dwellings of single family and 2 family buildings. There was a funeral home converted from a single family or 2 family building on the south side of Pavilion Street, east of Wooster. It was called "Johnson's Funeral home."

I was at the dedication of Bellevue Square when it opened in 1941. Reverend Hopes was the pastor of Bethel A.M.E. Church. He was very instrumental in getting that project built. He lived on the corner of Clark and Westland Street. Bethel was on Winthrop Street. It burned down. Then they moved to a building on Bellevue Street for a while. Then they moved to that old synagogue on Main Street, next to the Masonic Lodge. Then they had a split in the congregation. Some of them stayed there and some of them went in with the Talcott Street Congregation and they bought that building where Faith Congregational Church is across the street from Metropolitan A.M.E. Zion. The area where Mary Sheppard Place is now (formerly Bellevue Square) consisted primarily of multiple tenement buildings, small houses, mom and pop stores, fish markets etcetera. They tore that whole area down between Wooster, Bellevue, Pavilion and Canton. However, they only tore down one side of Canton and one side of Pavilion, so some of the buildings remained on those streets after Bellevue Square was built. Some friends of mine used to go in those old buildings that were being demolished, and take all of the copper, brass and lead out of them. They would sell the scrap and always had fat pockets in school.

My family never moved into Bellevue Square because my father wouldn't have it. He couldn't understand why they would put so many black people in one place like that. To the best of my knowledge, there was never a white family in there. Mahoney Village, which was on Vine Street across from Mather, never had any blacks in it. Nelton Court had only one or two black families in it. Actually, the father of one of the families was black and the mother was white. His name was Pete Smith and he was a World War 1 veteran. He met his wife in France during the war and married her there. Then he came here and raised a family while living in Nelton Court. We used to call him "Cousin Pete". However, he was not a relative. My father had two sets of relatives, Cousin Mary Lizzie whose husband looked white, and the Slappy's. They were on his side of the family. They were very nice people who also lived on Wooster Street too. The other projects were black and white.

When Bellevue Square was built there were around 500 units in the project. The footprint of Mary Sheppard Place covers the same land that Bellevue Square covered but some of the buildings came down. Mary Sheppard was the mother of someone I know, Rufus Sheppard. My friend O. C. Killens was either the 3rd or 4th family to move in there. Before the project was built, there were tenement buildings and small ma and pa stores along Wooster, Bellevue, and Pavilion Streets. So, Johnson's funeral home which originally was a single family house was torn down and it had to go to Main Street next to where Faith Congregational

Church is. Around the year 1939, the Johnson's Funeral home opened up at its new location on Main Street. They gave tours and described things like how to embalm people. At the time it was state of the art. Believe it or not, he actually put a restaurant in the building called "ye old log cabin." It was on the other side of the funeral home on the side closest to where Faith Congregational Church is now. Eventually, it became James' Funeral Home. Then a guy by the name of Lewis had it.

Wooster Street

Wooster Street, north of Pavilion looks a lot like it did when I was a kid. There have been a few changes. . If you stood on the northeast corner of Wooster and Pavilion and looked north you had Hopewell Baptist Church, Snyders Grocery Store, two apartment buildings and a Hebrew Funeral home right across the street from Faith Congregational Church's parking lot. My house was 2 houses north of where the funeral home was on the same side of the street. On Suffield Street at the northern end of Wooster Street there used to be a Jewish synagogue. That's where Mount Olive moved to after they left Bellevue Street.

If you stood at the southwest corner of Wooster Street and Pavilion there was a residential building. After that, there was Sam Rappaport's grocery store and a group of 3 story brick buildings on the west side. Sam Rappaport owned some of those apartment buildings.

I took the census in my neighborhood in 1950. I was responsible for Main to Canton, the west side of Wooster Street to Suffield and back up to Main Street all the way to Canton. My area included the buildings across the street from "Old North Cemetery". There were widows living there and the buildings were actually called "the widows home". Someone by the name of "Ives" donated the land where the buildings still stand. All of the women living in there were white. There weren't any blacks living in there. They all had electric stoves; they were not allowed to have gas stoves because if you turned the stove on and it didn't light, you could be killed by the gas. Glazers grocery store was south of Pavilion on the east side of Wooster.

Bellevue Street

Prior to the hurricane of 1938 there were many trees along Bellevue Street that no longer exist. Elm trees in particular. There were horse chestnut trees. One of them was in the side yard of my wife Agnes' house which was on Wooster Street. We used to throw sticks to knock them down. They were lime green and they would fall off by themselves. When they fell they were covered by something that looks like spikes. When it ripened, it would open up and a chestnut would be inside. There were a lot of them in Hartford along with the umbrella trees that used to grow Indian Cigars. We used to dry them out so that we could try and smoke them. The Italians used to love them for the shade that they produced. We used to have one on Garden Street along with weeping willow trees in my back yard. When my father died, my mother had them cut down because the roots of these trees were good at finding water and they would get in the plumbing and crack foundations.

There were also many businesses along Bellevue Street. Bellevue Street started at Canton Street and went all the way to Sanford Street. Going north down Bellevue Street from Pavilion there was a large 6 family apartment building. It stood on the corner of Bellevue and Blake Streets. In that building there were stores on the first floor and apartments up above. Other buildings on that street were designed the same way. On the same side of the street were a barber shop, a grocery store, and further down there was a grocery store owned by an Italian guy. Next to that was a package store owned by a black guy named Carl La Sear. Next to that (I believe 202) was another building where Bernie Harris, Claudia Gomes and Claudia's daughter, Beverly Gomes lived. Bernie Harris was Steve Harris' Father. After that it looked pretty much the way it looks now except there were 2 or three, three family structures there. Then came Suffield Street.

Right on the northeast corner of Suffield (now Battles) and Bellevue was a drug store owned by a man named Weinstein. There were apartments upstairs. Next to that on the first floor was Mr. McIver's grocery store. He was the brother-in-law of L. B. Barnes (the funeral director). L. B. Barnes was married to his sister. Three buildings north of the drug store was a shoemaker shop run by a man named Pete. Most of these stores were on the bottom floors of dwelling units. The next street was Warren Street. In between Warren Street and Loomis Street was the Walter G. Camp School. Years later it would be renamed "Arsenal Annex". There were other buildings before the Walter G. Camp School, and one on the corner after it. The back yard of the school went all the way to Windsor Street. That's where the playground is now. The building now known as the Willie Ware Center was not there when I was a kid. When my grandmother stayed at 21 Loomis Street, the school yard was part of the back yard of my grandmother's housed. Kids who were underweight and probably had tuberculosis went to school there. When that school was closed down some of the kids came to Arsenal on Main Street and the others went to Bracket on Westland Street. That school was closed by the time WWII came. After that it was used as a training school related to the war effort.

Blake Street

Blake Street no longer exists because the name of it was changed to Pavilion Street. To get there when I was a kid you had start at Main Street and go down Pavilion Street for 2 blocks to where it ended at Bellevue Street. When it ended at Bellevue Street you could take a quick left and then a right and you would be on Blake Street. Blake Street was just one block long and it went from Bellevue Street to Windsor Street. Blake Street used to be much steeper than it is now. It didn't used to have a curve in it like it does; it was straight from Bellevue Street to the train tracks. I used to sled down it in the winter time. I'm surprised that no one got killed on it because we used to play on it. I remember someone pushed me down that hill in a big tire like a damn fool. The tire hit the curb on the other side of Windsor Street. I never did that again, you never need to do that more than once.

Going south on Bellevue from Pavilion you had the following: on the left was the Aetna brewery. I believe there were actually two breweries in that area at the time and one of them made Dover Beer. There was also a beer called Red Fox Ale. If you look in that area you will see a smoke stack, that used to have the name "Aetna" painted on it. I think I know who owned that brewery during the 1940's. I know he had it during the Circus Fire of July 1944 because I remember helping a guy out named Lee Williams. His father owned trucks and used to run deliveries for the brewery owner. I remember going with him to deliver beer to different places like restaurants and the invoice would say five cases. I shouldn't have been touching the stuff because I was only 18 and you had to be 21 back then to drink. It's strange to think that we could be drafted at 18 but we couldn't drink alcohol. After a while that law changed. Well the owner or manager of the restaurant would say "I didn't order five cases of this swill, take it back." Well the brewery owner would tell Lee to take it back and leave it in front of the owner or managers business. Lee would then say, "well who's going to sign for it?"

The brewery owner would then say, "we don't' need a signature just leave it in front of his place, he'll take it in." The brewery owner asked me, "What are you doing this for?" (Helping to deliver beer?). I answered, "I just got out of high school, I can't find a job, and I need some money so I'm helping this guy (Lee Williams). I'm in the draft for the army or navy or whatever". He said, "when you get out come back and see me." However, when I got out he was dead. He died prior to my discharge from the Navy. He was something. At one time he was the political boss of the democratic side. This brewery owner, ran the city. Years later I found out.

I only worked helping to deliver beer for a little while because in August I went into the military. Somewhere in that immediate area around Bellevue and Blake Street, there was a chicken market named Segals that sold live poultry. Next to the brewery was a restaurant, a bakery and some 6 or 12 unit apartment buildings. On the north east corner of Blake Street was a big apartment building which went almost all the way to Windsor Street. Seabrook Ice cream was right on the corner of Windsor and Blake Streets, after the apartment building. I believe the Seabrook Ice Cream building is still there and the CRT operates a division out of it.

Windsor Street

Starting from Terry Square traveling south on the east side of the street there was a tobacco warehoused. That building is still standing today on the corner of Windsor Street and Boce Barlow Way. There was also a factory named Cushman Chuck. Then there was another factory. Then there was a meat packer and another tobacco warehouse. That's the way it looked on the east side of Windsor Street up to Suffield Street. The rest was railroad yard all the way up to Canton Street and beyond.

On the west side going south from Terry Square there was the Terry Square Restaurant and another business where the other restaurant (the one facing Windsor Street) now stands. There was another business there but I cannot recall what it was. After that, Hartford Electric Light had some equipment that included a power station with transformers. It's still there. Then there was a business that I cannot recall the name of. After that was Hartford Stove, Blue Bell Mattress and Superior Spring. Then came the rag shop that's now an auto junk yard. Mack Truck was on the corner of Sanford Street. At Loomis Street was the chicken market, then there were houses up to Suffield Street. Then there was Hartford House Wrecking. This was a place that would take a building apart and sell whatever they could reclaim to people, like doors and the sort. Then there was another brewery (not Aetna). On the northwest corner of Blake and Windsor Street was Seabrook Ice cream. That building is still there and is occupied by CRT (the Community Renewal Team).

After Bellevue Square was built in 1941, the land after that was occupied by the Hartford Housing Authority. It was in that year that the trolley's stopped running and they were replaced by busses. We used to pay for the trolley with tokens. You could get 3 tokens for twenty five cents. Each token could get you anywhere the busses ran, including a transfer. In 1942 and 1943 they took up the tracks for the trolleys so that they could use the iron for the war effort. During those days they collected practically everything including the tin foil found in cigarette wrappers. Although tin foil was used to keep the cigarettes fresh, the foil was removed and never seen again. For the war effort the U.S. Government used to sell war bonds. They also sold stamps in school to the students. The lowest denomination, I believe, was a dime. After you purchased your stamps, you would put them in a book until you got $18.75 worth. When the bond matured in ten years, it would be worth $25.00.

On the corner of Windsor and Canton Streets, they had an incinerator building that was used to burn the garbage for all of the residents of Bellevue Square, and the heating plant for Bellevue Square.

Between Avon and Pleasant Street was the original Cozy Spot. When they tore Windsor Street down that's when the Cozy Spot moved to Barbour Street. Norris Graves (the Real Estate Manager and original owner of Norris's Barber shop) his aunt and uncle owned the Cozy Spot when it was on Windsor Street and when it was moved to Barbour Street.

Canton Street

The Elks Club was at 59 Canton Street, on the south side of the street. At the end of Canton and Windsor Street was a package store.

Jennings Road

Boce Barlow Way turns into Jennings Road at Weston Street. From there it goes all the way to the old Hartford Police Headquarters. Jennings road was named after a Black police officer named Henry Jennings who lost his life in the line of duty in May of 1964, at the Hartford Hotel. I cannot remember the name of the person the police were looking for. He had done something. I don't know if he had killed somebody or not. Officer Jennings went in the Hotel to see if the person was there and if so, to arrest him because the detectives were on his trail. Although there were plain clothed detectives on the scene, Officer Jennings was sent in, in spite of the fact that he had on his uniform. The person he was looking for spotted Officer Jennings and killed him with one shot.

The Walter G. Camp School went from Bellevue to Windsor Street. At one time it was called the Arsenal Annex. If you know where the Willie Ware Center is, then you know the Eastern boundary of the school. My grandma moved to 21 Loomis Street. Her back yard went right into the yard of the Walter G. Camp School. After they stopped using it as one of the regular schools in Hartford they used it for kids who were recuperating from tuberculosis. Kids who lived between Suffield and Sanford Street attended that school after the consolidation of 1936. The kids from Wooster Street went to Northeast which was on Westland Street. The kids from Canton Street went to the Henry Barnard Junior High School which was on Main Street on the West, Ely Street on the North, Winthrop Street on the East and Pleasant Street on the South. Barnard School became Barnard Brown when the Brown School was torn down on Morgan Street.

The Brown School once stood at the location of Morgan and Market Streets. The Police Department Headquarters was at that same location following the close of the school. I'm not sure if the police headquarters was in a different building or if it was in the old Brown School but the police headquarters used to have a full basketball court in it and the Police Athletic League (PAL).

One block East of Market Street used to be Hartford's Connecticut Boulevard which used to run north and south along the Connecticut River. That's where they used to distribute the food for the needy during the Great Depression. I-84 went through there and took all of that out. Where that jail was, the streetscape and the bridge now stand.

1936, the year of "The Flood"

It was a common thing to have spring flooding in the Meadows every year. That's where the Post Office now stands. My grandmother lived in a six unit apartment building at 51-53 Sanford Street during the flood of 36. The left side of the building was 53 and the right side was 51. She lived in the 53 side. The water literally covered Windsor Street, South to the State Theater, North to Terry Square and my grandmother's basement. She came and stayed with us on Wooster Street when it happened. It also covered all of Bushnell Park and Colt Park with water. It was partially caused by the melting of the snow that fell during the winter.

If you planted a garden in "the Meadows" on a regular basis, eventually you would own the land. You then could then commercialize it and it would then go on the tax rolls. In other words, it was like "Homesteading". Prior to the dyke being built around 1941, the drive-in theater and the bowling alley that once occupied the Meadows would not have been feasible. Now, that property is more valuable than Downtown Main Street. Nowadays some of the finest car dealerships in the country are located there. Being on the Board of Assessment and Appeals since the mid 1980's, I have had a lot of interaction with people regarding matters of this type.

No TV-No Problem

Long before the days of television, we occupied our time in a variety of ways. We had to be at home when my father came home from work which was 5 o'clock. That was dinner time. Everybody was at that table for dinner at the same time, except for me. I didn't have to be home because I was selling newspapers, the Hartford Times. However, when I got home my meal would be waiting for me. That was almost all the way through until we got grown. No one else worked like I did. My sister Thelma worked later on in high school cleaning houses in the Westland and Garden Street area.

My brother Charlie did after school stuff. He wanted to play football but he had a heart murmur back then, at the age of 17. He wanted me to sign the permission slip so that he could play anyway but I wouldn't sign it. If something had happened to him my mother would have probably killed me. Charlie was her favorite son. He was the one that hung around when he was a little kid. He was always holding on to her.

Our neighborhood was our street actually. We didn't wander because we had everything in our neighborhood. We had the Independent Social Center on Main Street near Suffield Street, one block from where we lived. We had the church yard behind Faith Congregational Church. We used to play ball in there on the asphalt. We would play baseball with a tennis ball. We also used to play on the grass of Union Baptist Church's yard. At Metropolitan, next to Spring Grove Cemetery, they had a playground in the back with a seesaw, a swing and they had this thing that was like an Ariel seesaw.

It was up about 6 feet so you had to jump up to grab it with both hands. When your feet hit the ground you could jump and that would allow someone to grab the other end. Once you got it started, the two of you could keep it going like a seesaw without either of you hitting the ground. Once in a while someone would get on top of it and run from one end to the other. We played on that thing with no supervision. It's a wonder it didn't kill somebody.

Once in a while a ball would get in one of the gutters of the Windsor Avenue Congregational church (now known as Faith Congregational). The roof had and still has around a 30 degree pitch.

However, there were kids in our neighborhood that could climb on to the roof and then they would climb down to the gutter and throw the balls out. They would get on the roof by climbing on to an overhang that was on the north side of the building. Then they would scale along the roof until they got over the balls in the gutter. The roof was made of slate and there were eyelets that were between the sections of slate. The eyelets extended above the roofs surface so that the kids could grab them as they descended the roof. Well, some kids would access the roof at almost the roofs peak. Once they got above the balls in the gutter they would climb down to the gutter and throw those balls down. As soon as they threw the balls down, we would immediately restart the game.

There was a Polish kid up the street, we called him Skintzel. Every time we got a ball caught in the gutter we would get Skintzel over there and he would walk up the steps to the overhang, then he would get on top of the roof and go down to the gutter holding onto those eyelets. If one came loose God only help him because he was a lightweight, he couldn't have weighed more than 130 pounds. If it sounds strange for me to mention a Polish kid in my neighborhood, remember, when I was a little kid we (blacks) were in the minority on Wooster Street. It was mostly White. The Marrotta's used to live across the street from us, the ones who used to do the auto shows at the Civic Center and the car races. Frank Marrotta's son was the one responsible for the light show at Goodwin Park.

My friend Tom Jenkins and I used to wrestle on the grass in front of the Church until he got too strong for me. The last time I wrestled with him it was a draw. I said to myself "no more, it doesn't make sense, I can never win again." We were about the same size and I was about 6 months older than Tom but he got much stronger.

The executive director of the Independent Social Center was Samuel Jenkins, and the second in charge was Frank T. Simpson Sr. He did a lot of work for the fair employment practice commission. The Simpson/Waverly school on Waverly Street is named after him. His son also worked for the State as an architect or an engineer. He is retired now. The Social Center ran Camp Bennett which was out in Glastonbury. Although I went there, I never stayed there overnight. Even when we got grown they used to have social events there. They used to have hay rides out there too.

They used to have camping overnight for 5 dollars per week. That was for day camp, overnight boarding and 3 meals a day. The Community Chess helped support Camp Bennett. It consisted of the old line wasp families like Fletcher Parker who was a minister and Alfred Fuller of Fuller Brush fame. They were donors primarily to keep yawl out of the YMCA downtown. Nobody in my family went to Camp Bennett to stay. There was no such thing as 5 dollars per week for us to go to camp. But, I used to go to the Social Center and we used to have Bible school there and at A.M.E. Zion Church during the summer time. That's where I learned to take pictures and develop them from Willie DeLoach. We would have this Kodak camera and we would develop the pictures we took. The camera and all the developing equipment probably belonged to him. We would take photos of us and things in the neighborhood. We would take the film back to the center and put them through a 3 part process; a developer, a fixer and a washer. I could actually see the pictures come out. It was an amazing process. You had an ultraviolet light which is a black light so that you don't over expose the photo. Then we would go over to the basement of A.M.E. Zion Church and watch 16 millimeter movies like the "our gang comedies", Laurel and Hardy and stuff.

Up until the early 40's there were two sisters that lived across the street from me on Wooster Street. They lived in the same building where my wife, Agnes, used to live. They were bootleggers. Mrs. Lamar lived on the second floor at 149 and Mrs. Nighton lived underneath Agnes on the 1st floor at 151. They used to sell whisky after hours and on Sunday. There was a steady parade of people marching in and out of that building.

The Independent Social Center actually consisted of 2 buildings in my neighborhood. One was on Main Street and the other was on Wooster Street north of 149-151 on the same side of the street. Both of them are gone. At one time they owned the whole corner of Suffield and Main Street. Suffield Street is now known as Battles Street. Some of the buildings were residential. There was also a store in one of the buildings that they eventually owned on the corner of Main and Suffield. There is a building that the A.M.E. Zion church still owns and uses next door to where the Independent Social Center once stood. There's currently a sign on it. It's a single family building that is diagonally across from A.M.E. Zion. It used to be a parish for the minister.

No Time for Leisure

There was a Boys' Club in my neighborhood. It stood at the corner of Ely and Winthrop Streets, and was known as the Goodwill Boys Club. Although the Goodwill Boys Club was just a few blocks from my housed, I never went there. I spent my time after school and on Saturday selling *The Hartford Times.* It was the afternoon newspaper. I would get out of school, go home to 158-160 Wooster Street, walk downtown to the Times building on Prospect Street, pay 2 cents for each paper I intended to sell and then I would go to Main Street in front of Sage Allen's Department Store. I would sell each paper for 3 cents which would mean that I made a penny profit each time I sold one. Sometimes I would meet somebody rich or generous and they would give me a nickel and say "here, keep the change." I did this from the age of eleven until I was fifteen years old.

School History

I attended Arsenal School from the age of 5 until I was 12 (1931-1938). Arsenal School was at 1800 Main Street and was surrounded by Wooster Street on the East, the Widows homes buildings on the north and Canton Street on the south. There was a building in between the school and Canton Street on the same side of the street. On the northeast corner of Canton and Main Streets was a drug store owned by Jake Hyman. He may have owned the building. It was actually more on Canton than Main. The doorway was on the Canton Street side. It was in a building that you had to walk up two or three steps to get to. Cecil Davis had a restaurant there at one time, Mr. Wilson had a small bodega that carried a little of everything. His daughter Betty was in my wife, Agnes' Weaver High graduating class. Up above were residences and doctors offices. Dr. Howard Warring was there and so was Dr. Dixon the dentist. These were black Doctors. Arsenal School was directly across the street from "Old North Cemetery" and some of the students used to get flowers from the grave sites and give them to their teachers. Somehow, the teachers found out and from then on, the flowers went in the waste basket. After Arsenal School, I attended Northeast Junior High on Westland Street from age thirteen to fifteen (1938-1941). I know the year that I began school at Northeast Junior High because during my first semester there, the following happened to me:

I was still selling newspapers downtown. I lived just a couple of blocks from my school but in

September of 1938, I got wet going to school because it was raining real hard. I got excused from school early because I wanted to go home, change into some dry clothes and continue on to sell newspapers. After I changed clothes, I had to go from my house on Wooster Street to *The Hartford Times* building on Prospect Street and sell the early edition if possible. *The Hartford Times* had several editions believe it or not. They had the "mail edition" that came out at 11:30 in the morning, that's the one that they put on the trains and sent out of town. Then they had one at around 12:30 or 1:00. Then they had the 2:30 edition and then the Wall Street at 4:25 or 4:30. That was the final edition. That's the one that I sold every day except for Saturdays. After I got my papers, I would go to Main Street in front of Sage Allen's Department Store. That day, I could not sell papers on the street because as I started selling my papers, I got caught in the hurricane of 1938. As I tried to sell my papers a woman begged me to seek shelter so I went into the Loews Poli Theater. It used to be known as the Capital Theatre during the 1930's. I stayed there until the winds subsided. She was right too; I could have gotten killed out there. I couldn't sell any papers in there either because everybody had left.

A Witness to History

When I was a kid, parades used to come all the way up Main Street to the Spring Grove Cemetery. I used to watch them at the intersection of Main and Pavilion Streets. One of my earliest recollections includes seeing Civil War Veterans. In 1935, I used to see them riding in cars during the parades in Hartford. They would have had to have been almost 90 years old at the time but I saw them. I also remember Spanish American War Veterans from the war that was fought in 1898. My Aunt Nanny's, husband's cousin "old Ike Terry", was a veteran of that war. There were a lot of WWI Veterans in those parades. I remember them with their leggings on. Black people have fought and died in every war this nation has ever had.

As a child I read consistently, because we didn't have the money to go anywhere, our books took us where we wanted to go. We had two libraries in our neighborhood; one called the Ropkins Branch was located on Main Street close to where the Keney Clock Tower is, and the other was on Main Street close to where Crane Court is today. We didn't have television back then so in addition to my homework assignments I read three more books per week. At one time I vowed to read all of the books in the library. I didn't know that there were many more libraries other than the ones in my neighborhood.

Here I am at the age of 12. That's how I dressed every day for school, and the way I was dressed when I was selling papers downtown. I think I got the hat from one of my uncles. I took this picture from a machine in one of the stores downtown. To get one you had to go into a booth, pull the curtain and insert a dime. Although, it came with a frame, a dime was a lot of money for me.

I had to sell ten papers to make a dime back then. I usually sold 25 papers per day. If I didn't sell them I still had to pay for them. However, if I thought I couldn't sell them I would go to Jake's newsstand at the corner of Main and Asylum. He would take the ones that I could not sell and give me 2 cents apiece for them.

Prior to my attending Northeast Junior High, the school was divided into Bracket and Northeast Junior High. Prior to my going there, Bracket was a school that went from the kindergarten to the 8th grade and then you would go from there to high school. However, around 1937, there was a consolidation of schools in Hartford. That meant Bracket would go from the kindergarten to the 6th grade, and Northeast would go from the 7th to the 9th. I went to Northeast after the consolidation, so I went there from the 7th to the 9th grades. I remember my first day of school. My mother bought me a corduroy suit and that's what I wore. Back then we wore a tie every day to school so being in a suit wasn't that unusual. After Northeast I went to Weaver High. I wore a tie to Weaver high school every day and sometimes I even wore a bow tie, the kind you had to tie yourself. That was the only kind that I would wear. Only the sissies wore the clip on kind. That's how I learned to tie a bow tie. It would always get crooked and the girls would straighten it out. Weaver High school was on Ridgefield Street, named after Thomas Snell Weaver. I went there with the class of 44'. When I went there, the school was around forty-five percent Jewish. A Jewish Holiday would empty the school. Weaver and Bulkeley High School, which was in the South End of Hartford, came into existence in the same year, 1923. Prior to that, there was only one high school in Hartford, Hartford High. It was one of the oldest Public Schools in the Country. I went right from Weaver High to the service during WWII.

Church History

I never went to Union Baptist Church. The people who went to Union Baptist Church lived on the west side of the trolly tracks that went down Main Street. They lived on streets like Mahl Avenue and Pliny Street. We had our own cast system. I didn't know them.

Faith Congregational Church was not in the picture in those days because it was a white church when I was a kid. It was known as "Windsor Avenue Congregational Church". The Hillyers went there at some point and time because there are plaques inside the church to show the stuff that they donated. Most of the front line families (those people who originally lived in the area) went to Mount Olive, Hopewell, and Mount Calvary, although my Church (Mount Calvary) was downtown at the time, on Charter Oak Avenue near Governor Street (now Popolewskew Court). As I grew older and went to Weaver High School I got to know people from the other side of the trolley tracks that ran down Main Street, because many of the students at Weaver were from those areas. The people who lived on Pliny Street and south of Pliny went to Hartford High but the people who lived east of the trolley car tracks from Mather Street north went to Weaver. Everyone north of Pavilion Street, Mahl Avenue and Ridgefield Street went to Weaver High School. Many of the people south of those streets went to Hartford High school. Canton Street was the cutoff line on the east side of the trolly track.

The culture at Hartford High was very different from Weaver High. Hartford High had a lot of Italians and Pole's. Weaver was mostly Jews, Irish and a few Blacks. We didn't have any Puerto Ricans in those days. Buckley had only a few Blacks that went there. The only Blacks that I knew of that went to Bulkeley was the Walkers on Roosevelt Street and the Burgeses.

Bethel A.M.E. had a church on Winthrop Street but it burned down in a fire. They had a building at about 210 Bellevue Street where they held services first, before they moved to Main Street. Eventually, they got the one at 2003 Main Street. That building used to be a synagogue or workman's center. They are in Bloomfield now. They reconfigured the façade to make it look like a church. That was once a dwelling and the Jews turned it into a workman's center which was like a club or social center. Bethel had a split among their membership. So, when the split came, half of them joined Talcott Street Congregational and then they formed Faith Congregational Church.

Faith had not owned the church on Main Street for very long. Before it moved to Main Street it was on Talcott Street. Talcott Street Congregational was on Talcott Street until the early 1950's. The reverend that I knew from there was Reverend Wright. When they moved to Main Street, Reverend Wright was still the pastor. Talcott Street Congregational was the oldest Black Church in Hartford. Maybe in Connecticut I don't know.

The Church Fires

Faith Congregational Church caught fire one night, the same night that another church in Hartford burned. Both edifices burned the same night. It was probably Saint Joseph's Cathedral. I believe this happened after Faith moved from Talcott Street. It must have been arson. Two churches the same night? The guy was on the move. This fire had to be in the late 50's because there were two properties that G. Fox's did not have near their building; Talcott Street Congregational Church and Youth Center, which was a children's clothing store right on the corner of Talcott and Main Street, butted right up against G. Fox. That building is still there. Eventually, they got Faith because they put their garage there. When Cliff Bunkley died that was the first funeral that I went to in Faith Congregational Church on Main Street. His family belonged to Talcott Street Congregational Church originally.

Metropolitan AME Zion Church goes back to 1833. That church is over 175 years old. They were on the corner of Pearl and Ann Streets at one time where the firehouse is. That was their property until 1925. There are one or two people still in that church from Pearl Street. Marge Abbott is one of them and Rachael Richardson, who just turned 100 this year. They were both "Pearl Streeter's". I don't know anybody else. Miss Tillman probably was one, she lived to be 114. Rachael hit a hundred this year and Marge is probably 95 or 96, because Marge is 8 or 10 years older than I am and still walking around. Rachael is a good musician. She was the organist at Metropolitan.

Jean Brown from Mahl Avenue played piano too, if my memory serves me correctly. Her brother, Gordy Brown, played tenor sax and her father, Raymond Brown, played trombone. I remember seeing Gordy perform. I don't remember the Browns living at any place but 29 Mahl Avenue. I remember the number because they were on the left hand side going down. It's a 2 family building. Gordy and I were real friendly. We were in the same class. Your wife's grandfather may have been a Mason at Excelsior Lodge. They were very exclusive back then, not everybody could get in. You had to live in the area. They blackballed more people than they let in there. That lodge used to meet at Union Baptist Church. Reverend Jackson was the pastor there when I was a kid. I don't know where they were before then. I don't know if they ever had a building before they moved into 2 Mahl Ave. Back when I was a kid the Jews owned the building where Excelsior Lodge is now. If you look at the east side of the building you will see a rounded part, that's where they kept the Torah. The ceiling separating the first floor from the second floor was not there at one time, but there was a railing that made it possible to walk around the outside of the second floor.

Television Comes to Hartford

I was around 13 when I saw my first television set. It was during a television broadcast at G. Fox on Main Street. I believe this was in 1939. I couldn't believe what I was seeing. The television was in one area and the television cameras were in another area. I kept running back and forth trying to catch something different between what was happening and what was showing on the television. They were broadcasting right there to demonstrate televisions to promote the selling of them. It was in the area where they had their appliances like radios. At the time, they didn't even have televisions to sell, just radios. If you remember, I bought a radio at Kaye's for thirty-nine dollars, one dollar a week. There was an outlet in the back of the radio for a T.V. connection. So when you bought a television, you were supposed to connect the television to the radio and sit the screen on top. It never happened because it doesn't make sense, but anything to sell stuff.

I found out about the television demonstration at G. Fox because I was always there selling papers. I used to run into G. Fox once in a while to get warm. That's how I found out. I also used to do a lot of window shopping and that was the greatest place in the world to go window shopping for a kid. They never bothered us because we didn't bother anything. We never even heard of shoplifting so we weren't thieves. We were always welcome. G. Fox was the only store that I know of where you could use the bathroom. It was clean, spacious and they had the best stuff in town. G. Fox was like Hartford's Macy's or Gimbel's. I knew one of the guys that drove the owner of G. Fox but I can't think of his name. Tall brown skinned guy…had a brother. I think his brother murdered somebody.

Of course, all of the blacks that they hired were the same size, same color. I remember all of the elevator operators were the same color, 6 feet tall and the chief elevator operator was Charlie Berry. He was also in charge of the waiters at the Hartford Club. He used to take his lunch at G. Fox in time to work at the Hartford Club. After lunch he would go back to G. Fox. When his day was finished at G. Fox he would go work dinner at the Hartford Club. Basically, he had 2 full time jobs. He made a lot of money. He had Ms. Arubach (the owner of G. Fox) as a connection. That was connection enough. However, there weren't any

Jewish members of the Hartford Club. Not in those days. "No sir re Bob". I believe the first Jewish person to be asked to join was Governor Abraham Ribbicoff and he wouldn't go there. In those days, the governor of the state would have lunch at the Hartford Club on the day of his inauguration. Ribbicoff, being the first Jewish person elected to the office of governor wouldn't have his there. He had his at the Hartford Hilton when it was on Ford Street.

Governor Cross was an old man when he was called out of retirement to run for governor again. He used to sleep in the back of his limousine. He actually lived at the Hartford Club. I don't believe the state owned the Governor's Mansion on Prospect Avenue at that time.

    In 1940, I was 14 years old. I had a friend named Frank who lived on Wooster Street and he had a girlfriend who lived on Main Street, right across from the Lincoln Dairy. While she was at work, Frank would borrow her car and we would hang out together. Frank's father lived on the corner of Wooster and Suffield Streets. Franks father had a car also, and to use his car Frank and I would push it out of the driveway and roll it down Suffield Street. When we got far away from the house, Frank would start it up. We would be on our way in a 1935 Studebaker President. It was a four door sedan with great springs on it. It rode like a baby carriage. I'd go with anybody who had a ride. If it wasn't for those rides I seldom went anywhere to hang out except in the area between Suffield and Pavilion Street. However, if I wanted to play tackle football, I had to go to Keney Park. One day after playing a game I walked home. I don't remember leaving the park or walking home until I got to Spring Grove Cemetery on Capen Street. I must have had a concussion and didn't know it. I wasn't about to tell anyone because back then if they sent you to the hospital you didn't come back. In those days, the city of Hartford ran the hospital. It was in the building that now stands at 2 Holcomb Street and it was called Municipal Hospital. That's where I had my tonsils out when I was nine or ten year old. I had to walk home because my mother came to pick me up on the trolley. Trolleys made me sick so I walked whenever I could. The trolley ran wherever you see the busses run today. Even on State Street which used to be a cobblestone street. Sometime during the war effort the tracks were taken up. With very few exceptions there are no trolley car tracks left in the streets of Hartford.

The 1940 World's Fair

In 1940, I was in the 9th grade. I was 14. It was in that year that my mother, Pearl Smith, brought me and my cousin, Mary Elizabeth King, and her husband Sam King, to the World's Fair in New York. Round trip by train cost 2 dollars. Back then, people worked for one or two dollars a day so that was a lot of money. My mother believed in meaningful entertainment for us. She used to pay two dollars a season for the school to bring us to the Bushnell Memorial, so that we could see shows like Hansel and Gretel.

High school in those days went from the 10th grade to the 12th. I can clearly remember my sophomore year at Weaver in 1941. I was there when the Japanese bombed Pearl Harbor. Basically, we didn't have any problems at Weaver. It was a good time to go to school. Some of my first teachers were Miss Moses for English, Mr. Lund for Biology and Physiology, Miss Craig who was an English teacher, and Miss Mansfield for American History. My years at Weaver were kind of uneventful because everything was gearing up for the war.

That's me in 1944

And here's my school. Weaver High, 1944

Mr. Jasper Howard

Jasper Howard was the only Black person working at Weaver at that time. You had to go by him if you came to school late. He would give you a slip of paper, so that you could enter the school. Jasper "Jenkins" the organ player was named after Mr. Howard because Mr. Howard was his Uncle. Jasper Howard's job was to give out "late slips" to students when they showed up late for school. I believe he was one of the founders of Hopewell Baptist Church which was in the church currently on the corner of Wooster and Pavilion Street.

This Church later became Holy Trinity. The building where the church is was once an apartment building. I believe it was a 6 tenement apartment building or maybe 12. At one time, the minister stayed on the top floor. The first minister that I remember from there was by the name of Crutchfield. That goes back to the early 1930's. The people who founded Hopewell came out of Mount Olive which was on Bellevue Street. Mount Olive moved to Suffield Street which is now Battles Street. The church originally was where part of Bellevue Square now is (Bellevue Square is now known as Mary Sheppard Park). The church was located down Bellevue Street near Canton on the East side of Bellevue Street, I believe.

The people who founded Mount Moriah came out of Hopewell. Hopewell moved to the corner of Enfield and Rockville Streets to an old Jewish Synagogue. Shortly after WWII, the Jews started moving out of Hartford to Bloomfield and West Hartford. Hopewell no longer is at the corner of Enfield and Rockville Streets. It is now on Windsor Avenue in Wilson at the old Shop-Rite supermarket. I remember all of this because I was there. I may not be able to remember what I had for breakfast but that stuff I remember. In any event, Mr. Howard's whole family went to Hopewell when it was located at the corner of Wooster and Pavilion Streets. When students addressed Jasper Howard they referred to him as "Jasper" everyone else was Miss or Mister somebody.

There were 13 Black guys in our class and 24 Black girls, because of the very large Jewish population in that part of the city. About forty percent of the students were Jewish. Whenever there was a Jewish Holiday, half the school was out. At that time academically, Weaver ranked right up there with some of the best schools in the country.

Agnes

I met my wife Agnes when I was very young. She and I lived across the street from each other when I lived on Wooster Street. Sometimes we would go to the movies. I stopped delivering papers in 1941 or 1942. After that I started working at the Laurel Fur Shop. I then worked at Wise Dress Shop on Church Street. I used to clean a guy's photo studio that was upstairs near where the Strand Theatre was. I was paid twenty five cents an hour. In the summer of 1943, before I graduated from high school, I kept a record of my expenses, and in that record it states that I spent fifty-five cents to see the show. If it cost that much to see a show, it must have been at the State Theatre where they had live performances because a regular show would cost around twenty-five or thirty-five cents. People like Duke Ellington, Count Basie or some other big band would frequently play there. At one point, I borrowed a nickel from George Blanks. George was the older brother of Clarence Blanks, the oil company owner. Clarence was known for being a hard worker. He had a paper route in the morning which caused him to get up at 4:00 A.M.; he would then go to school, and then he would work at McIver's store on Bellevue Street. Clarence worked there from junior high school all the way through high school. Mr. McIver was the brother-in-Law of the owner of the L.B. Barnes' funeral home. When Mr. McIver died, Clarence ended up owning the store. He ran it well for a while. Then he went into the oil business. Such a nice person as a kid and as a grown man, too.

My record also shows that I spent sixty-six cents to see a movie. Since it cost thirty cents to see a movie back then, I must have gone with someone else. I must have taken Agnes because I wouldn't go to the movies with anyone else. I met Agnes when we were both around eight or nine years old. She lived right across the street from me when I lived on Wooster Street. I remember us going somewhere together when we were both in junior high school at Northeast. We started dating when I was in high school and she was still in junior high. I was fifteen and she was fourteen. She was one year behind me in age and academically. She graduated from Weaver in the class of 1945.

This is a photo of my wife Agnes when she was just seventeen years old. We were married November 24th 1952. At the time that this story was written we had been married for sixty years. We have three wonderful children together, Sharon, Billy, and Finitia, 8 grandchildren, 8 great grandchildren, and a new edition, 1 great great grandchild.

Here I am with my wife Agnes, my youngest child Finitia, my son Billy, and my daughter Sharon. Agnes had just retired as a school teacher and we were at the VFW on Blue Hills Avenue in Bloomfield, CT. The year was 1994.

Hartford's Theatres

Hartford used to have over twelve theatres that I can remember. Most of them were located south of "The Tunnel."

The original "Tunnel" is where the train runs underground just north of the Kenney Clock Tower. Starting from "the Tunnel" there was the Liberty which became the Daly because it was named by a guy named Daly. We used to call it the "scratch house." Then they had "the Parsons" also known as the "Proven Pictures. After that it became Parsons again which had real actors and not just movies. On Village Street (which used to run off of Main Street) was the State Theatre. They had big bands there and movies. I saw them all there. After the bend in the street, where the highway now is, there was "the Strand Theatre" on the right. Then when you got down to State Street there was the "Regal" and the "Princess" Theatres. On Asylum Street you had "Allyn" Theatre and the "E.M. Lowes". Farther down Main Street, there was the Lowes Poli Palace and then the Lowes Poli, aka the Capital Theatre. This one was directly across from City Hall. Further down Main Street on the left near Charter Oak Avenue was the Crown Theatre, and down Park Street was the

Lyric Theatre. They had a dance hall above that theatre. The building is still there. On Albany Avenue they had the Lenox Theatre. On Farmington Avenue there was the Colonial Theatre.

One of Hartford's many movie theatres was the Strand. They played Warner Brothers movies. I don't remember the first time I stepped into the Strand Theatre. I was in it the day of the circus fire. Oddly enough I don't remember what was playing on that day either. However, I do remember some of the movies that I saw there. In 1949 or 1950, I saw a world premier movie in Hartford there. It was after I got back from the service. It was called "Colt 45" and it starred Randolph Scott. It premiered in Hartford because the Colt 45 was made here at Colt firearms. I also saw the fighting 69th there starring James Cagney and Pat O'Brien. It was about a New York infantry regiment that went to World War One.

The Lowes Poli theatre (which was across the street from City Hall) played Metro Goldwyn Meyer (MGM) movies. They were the "muckity mucks". The Daly theatre played Republic movies. These were cowboy movies primarily. Those moves came out every week. All those theatres are gone. We just got one back on

Columbus Boulevard which used to be called Front Street. It's called The Spotlight Theatre. I went there recently with my niece, Kim and my brother-in-law Thomas Hall to see, *42*, the movie about Jackie Robinson.

July 6th 1944-the Circus Fire

I got out of high school in June of 1944 and I was helping a guy named Lee Williams deliver beer for Aetna Brewery which used to distribute beer from Windsor Street. I probably would have gone to the circus that night if I could have snuck in, but I wasn't going to buy a ticket.

I had just graduated from Weaver High School and I was waiting to receive my draft notice for me to report to the service. Because I knew I was going in I couldn't find work. Who would hire you when they know it would be just a matter of weeks before you had to leave? So I used to kill time by going to places like the Strand Theater. If you can remember the Strand Theatre, you can remember downtown Hartford before the highway was built because that's where the Strand Theatre was, right where the highway crosses under Main Street. I was in the movies at the Strand Theater, just about directly across from a place called Mohegan Market and diagonally across the street from G. Foxes, when the fire started. Back then, just about all of the space in downtown Hartford was commercially utilized. I could hear all of the sirens but a fire at the circus was the last thing that I was thinking. I never heard of a fire at the circus. But when I got out, everyone with a truck was used to transport bodies to the State Armory on Broad Street. 168 people died. In those days the circus would come into town for just one day.

After the fire took place I was helping to deliver beer that was made at Aetna Brewery which was on Bellevue, Blake and Windsor Streets. While I worked there, public officials impounded the circus and would not let them leave Hartford. The railroad cars were still down on Windsor Street, at the bottom of Blake Street until after I went into the Navy. After the fire, while some of the performers tried to transport beer from the Aetna Brewery to their railroad cars, we stole some of their beer. We were on this truck and the guys from the circus took a hand cart and carried the beer over the railroad tracks. It was kind of hard to carry that hand truck over the tracks so they left the cart and carried two cases at a time to the rail road car. We offloaded one when the guy's back was turned so that he was walking toward the train. The remaining cases of beer were sitting there. So my friends and I helped ourselves. The circus fire was July 6th 1944 and I went into the service the very next month on August 17th of that year.

I'm certain that when I left to go into the service, a month and a week later, those railroad cars were still there. I have no idea how they fed the animals, unless they let them out of here.

This is Windsor Street looking north from North Street. North Street used to run from Windsor to Front Street. The date is June 20th, 1941, less than 6 months before the U.S. entered WWII. The time is 10:05 A.M. In the background is the Aetna Brewery I spoke of earlier. Photo taken by Robert A. Gooch.

Here's a closer look at the Aetna Brewery. The Brewery was on Windsor Street between Blake and Canton. Photo taken by Robert A. Gooch.

This is Windsor Street, South of Pleasant Street. It was taken on the same day as the previous photos but at 10:05 A.M. The car on the left is going up Orchard Street which was one block north of where Trumbull Street is. Photo taken by Robert A. Gooch.

World War II

I was a sophomore at Weaver High school in 1941. One day, I was in front 149-151 Wooster Street, which was Tom Jenkins house across from where we lived at 158-160, and I was playing with Tom. Suddenly, my brother Charlie's friend, Pat Muse came running out yelling "the Japanese bombed Pearl Harbor." I remember wondering "what does that have to do with us." I didn't know. When we went to school on Monday, they had a general assembly and broadcasted live President Roosevelt's "the day that will live in infamy" speech. It was then that he asked for the declaration of war. The Jenkins family, were good people. I remember the day when I left home for war and Tom's mother was looking out the window crying. My mother was looking out of her window, too. For some unknown reason, I got to the draft board in New Haven and was told to come back the next day, which I did.

Once the United States entered the war, that's all we focused on. As a matter of fact, the war was what steered me. I wanted to have something that could help me while I was in the service and when I got out. I was a "right now person" not the kind of person who thought much about the future. So I wanted to study something that I could use in the service to keep me from being in a fox hole or marching all the damn time. I had no idea that I was going into the Navy, they threw me in the Navy. The draft board chose me to go into the Navy because they were filling quotas. Fortunately, or unfortunately, at the time the Navy's academic qualifications were higher than the Army's. That's probably why the draft board threw me in the Navy side. A fellow by the name of Willie B. McLendon, who has since passed away, he and I went together to take the test for the Air force. In those days it was not the United States Air Force, it was the Army Air Force because the Air Force was part of the Army. We went somewhere downtown. I always envisioned it being somewhere on Prospect Street. We took the test which took about 3 or 4 hours. Both of us thought we passed it. Out of 300 questions you only needed a score of 190. We both received notification that we didn't pass. We were both seniors in high school, but McLendon left High School and joined the Navy. He graduated but he left before our graduation ceremony.

Willie B. McLendon, 1944

I stayed and took the test to get into the Air Force again. This time they gave it at Weaver High School. The recruiter stated that we had a better chance of passing the test than students from states like Alabama and Mississippi because the academic standards in this part of the country were higher. This time I passed it. I then went to New Haven for the physical along with some other students. They paid for our transportation. I was the only black in the group. There was a policy at the time that if you were a senior in high school you could get an automatic deferral (they would not draft you) until your class graduated even if you were of draft age. At the physical examination, I started out with this group of other students from Weaver, going from one doctor to another one. At some point in time, they told me to take a seat. The rest of the students kept going. Then we broke for lunch. We all went to lunch together. When we came back, I sat. The rest of the students continued until the examinations were over. We left New Haven and came home. I knew that something was wrong. There was no way that I could get into the Air Force without taking the physical examination and I never went through the entire exam. When I got back to school and spoke with Principal Burke about this matter, his face got really red. He was really perturbed because he knew right off that I had been excluded. I never ever received notification about the outcome of that physical exam. I never got notified at all, nothing. That's when I asked him (Principal Burke) if I could be deferred until the class graduated. He said "no problem, I will take care of it." And he did. I never got another notice until my class graduated.

I graduated from Weaver High School in June of 1944 and was drafted in August of that same year. I didn't understand for a long time what had happened, but eventually I did. It wasn't that they were discriminating against me, it was that they could not facilitate me. There was only one place where they were training black pilots and that was Tuskegee and that was for blacks from all over the country. They had the cream of the crop. They didn't need kids 17 or 18 coming out of high school when they could get somebody right out of college.

There was only one person from Hartford who had made that program and that was Hartford's first Black policeman, Lemuel Custis. He went from the Hartford Police Department to the Army. He was in the first group of black pilots the United States Army Air Force ever had. His father was the receptionist for the President of the Aetna or the Travelers Insurance Company. In order to get to the president, you had to go through him. Lemuel was over qualified for everything he ever did. He was much over qualified to become a policeman. Nice guy too. He lived until 2005 and was living in Wethersfield when he died

I went in on the 18th of August, 1945. I was actually sworn in on the 17th, which was the day I went to New Haven and got sworn in. For whatever reason (I don't even remember the reason) they sent us back home and gave us tickets to report back the next day. Maybe they didn't have transportation or they weren't ready for us to go up to Great Lakes where I had my basic training. So I had to go back to New Haven and from there I went to Great Lakes. They told us to bring enough clothes for three days.

While going through training, I learned how to swim. We had to jump off of a tower about two stories high and swim for fifty yards. The reason why we had to do that is because if the ship sunk, it would take you down with it if you were too close to it. So you had to get away from it.

Here are my parents, Pearl and Benjamin Smith 1945. I was in the Navy when they took this photo and sent it to me. I was on the USS Dionysus at the time.

There was no such thing as someone going in from Hartford who could not read or write but I met plenty of people from other parts of the country in the Navy who couldn't read or write black and white. Because they filled their quotas just by sending bodies, Mississippi and places like that had citizens who could not read. I did meet people in the Navy other than black people who couldn't read, too. They were from Mississippi, Alabama and other southern states. I remember Mississippi right off the top of my head because when we were in boot camp in Great Lakes Illinois, right outside of Chicago, I used to write letters home for one of the guys that I liked very much by the name of George Squales.

A couple of guys that were in boot camp with me actually provided remedial training for people who could not read or write. With all of the things that we had to do, they found the time to do that. I don't understand how they did it. The races were segregated until after Franklin Roosevelt died and Harry Truman became President. That's when they desegregated the Navy. That's how I came to leave a segregated outfit in Manana Barracks in Hawaii, and was assigned to a ship in the Marshal Islands in the Pacific. It was one sad day when President Roosevelt died because we thought that he was the grand savior but it was Truman who integrated the Navy. Roosevelt could have done it but never did. As a matter of fact, if it was not for Mrs. Roosevelt, I doubt that the Tuskegee Airmen would have been allowed into the Air Force. She asked that a black pilot be allowed to fly her in a plane down in Tuskegee, Alabama. The Tuskegee Airmen were a grand experiment designed to fail. She went up in a plane with one of them and she said "he flies pretty well to me." If you can take the first lady of the United States off the ground and bring her back why can't you fly over Germany? Think about it. They turned out some of the best pilots in the world, ask the Germans or ask some of those bomber crews that they finally wound up escorting who didn't want them.

This is my Cousin Walter McBride in 1943. That was him on the left in the photo on page twenty-two with his mother and sister.

Back in the USA

After I came back from Japan to Seattle, Washington, we stayed across the bay from Seattle in Bremerton, Washington and Anchorage all winter from the end of November; we left in April. After staying in the Seattle area all winter, we went down to San Diego. The Captain may have had something to do with that because his home was in California. At that time I was getting closer and closer to the time when I had to decide if I wanted to be discharged or reenlist. From San Diego we went up to San Pedro, which was about 20 miles outside of Los Angles. That's where I stayed until my time was up. I was on board the ship all the while. Fortunately, once you go on board the ship you received additional pay called "sea pay." The sea pay was in there all the while I was overseas. Then it was time for me to be discharged. I went on a troop train from San Pedro, California to Lido Beach, New York. There were two sailors with me and I was in charge of them because I was a Petty Officer and they were not. The service always wanted to put somebody in charge of something. I got discharged in Lido Beach, New York. While I was in Lido Beach I ran into a guy who lived in New York I knew named Rudy

Simon, so I hung around with him and came on home to Hartford.

Hello Again Hartford

I was totally unready to be a civilian. I had nothing in mind but I did think that I could go back to school. For the first time in almost two years I didn't have anything to do or anywhere to go. It was actually frightening because I didn't know what to do with myself. For the past two years, I was at boot training, service school after that, processing sailors in Shoemaker California, and then with a repair ship that prepared for the invasion of Japan. Everyday, 24 hours a day, was filled up. I got home and had nothing to do. I went to the employment office and signed up for the "52/20 Club". That meant 20 dollars per week for 52 weeks if you don't have a job. Then I went and signed up for State Training School in Hartford. At the time there were no openings at the Hartford School, so me and a friend of mine signed up at Windham Regional Tech. I don't believe we stayed there an entire semester because a space opened up in Hartford and we transferred there.

The entire experience left me able to sympathize with a kid who has just graduated from college but cannot find a job. They get the training and education they need but nothings open to them. For them it must be difficult because they can't even draw unemployment. I didn't have a job either but there was a bill that provided the 20 dollars per week for 52 weeks for veterans.

While I was in school, Warren Stewart and I got jobs at night working at Plax Corporation. They were originally on the corner of Walnut and Edwards Street. They were a plastic manufacturer. They made milk bottles for babies. They didn't last because you couldn't sterilize them. However, they did a big business in White Walls which were plastic discs that you would place on a black car tire and it would turn the tire into whitewalls.

My brother, Charlie, used to take classes to become a printer at the Hartford Technical School on Washington Street known at that time as the "State Trade School". I attended that school in 1947-1949. I studied wiring and electric motor wiring. That school became the Hartford Adult Education Center. Bill Thompson was the head of that when he retired as Principal from Hartford High School sometime in the 1970's.

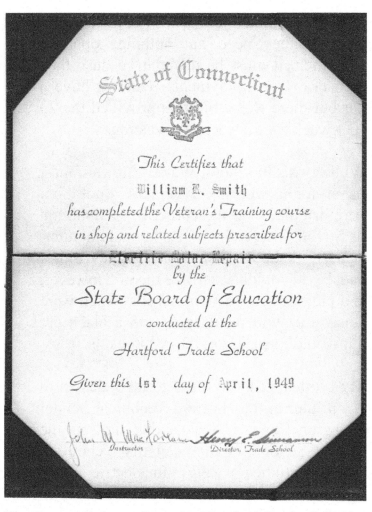

Here's my diploma from the Hartford Trade School. I graduated in April of 1949.

Socializing and Entertainment in my Neighborhood

*At one time entertainment was everywhere in Hartford...*William "Rab" Smith

I was 20 years old when I came home. In those days, you were supposed to be 21 to get into a nightclub. It was always strange to me that a person could go off to war but he couldn't go into a bar for a drink. However, nobody was checking I.D.'s. The calendar never stopped us from drinking anyway. We were drinking before we left at 16. Socializing meant renewing old friendships and hanging out with guys I knew before I went into the service.

The Sundown Nightclub was on Windsor Street next to East Avon Street. (Which was south of the Pallotti Underpass and where Canton Street is now). Roth Hardware, and the D and D Market, which is now on Franklin Avenue now, used to be in that block. Initially, Bill Cox owned the Sundown and somewhere down the line George Swan bought it. There were actually two nightclubs across from each other. The nightclub across the street was called "the Cotton Club". Prior to it being the Cotton Club, Jimmy Frazier's parents had it and it was a restaurant. I cannot remember what it was called but it was definitely a restaurant. So, eventually, George Swan owned both the Sundown and the Cotton Club which were directly across the street from one another. Horace Silvers (the jazz pianist, Walt Bolden (the drummer), Gene Nelson (another piano player) and Joe Calloway (the bass player) were all in and out of the Sundown and Stan Getz took them all away from here when he played the State Theatre. I'm not sure how long they performed with Getz but from that point on, they were residents and performers from New York.

At one time, Joe Calloway toured with Ella Fitzgerald. Everyone knew that Ella Fitzgerald did everything first class. Joe Calloway once told me that he was going on tour in Japan with Ella and he made arrangements to have his bass shipped to where they were going. When Ella heard of this she said "no you're not. Supposed it got lost or something what are you going to do, go and buy a Japanese bass?" So she bought a first class seat for his bass. Ella was first class all the way. Joe said that was the best job he ever had, playing for her. He once told me that Walt Bolden ended up teaching drums during the latter portion of his life. Horace Silvers is still around touring the United States and Europe, Gene Nelson has died. Gene came from a family of musicians in Hartford, they lived on Capen Street. Percy and Eugenia were the parents and they had three Sons; Percy Jr., Lenny and Gene. Gene was named after his mother. Percy Sr. was a hell of a reed man, he played all of the reeds but his specialty was alto saxophone. Percy Jr., was a piano player, he taught Gene. I don't think Lenny ever played. If so, I don't know about it. Percy Sr. was a hell of a man, nice guy too. He played at the old Bond Hotel on Asylum Street. Back then, blacks used to have to go in through the back. You could play in the lobby but you had to go in through the back. It was just like the Hartford Club on Prospect Street. Back then, they didn't have any blacks in the Hartford Club unless they were working. However, they did wind up having a black president. Richard Weaver-Bey was his name.

Around 1943, there was a band in Hartford led by Gene Nelson (Percy's Son). Gene played piano. They had a trumpet player named Joe Harris, a bass player named Joe Calloway and they had two drummers. One drummer was the brother of Donald Chafin, Jamie. Donald became a Captain in the Hartford Police Department. The other drummer was Walt Bolden. He used to play drums with the band off and on. Walt was the better drummer of the two. Hodge Davis played alto saxophone. They also had a saxophonist named Gordon Brown. I used to call him Gordy. Most of the guys in this band lived on Capen and Martin Street except for Hodge and Gordy. Hodge lived on Magnolia Street and Gordy and Joe lived on Mahl Avenue.

Mahl Avenue used to be two blocks long. It went from Main Street to Garden Street. Most of the houses on that street were two family houses. Blacks have lived on that street since I was a kid, although most of the people were white. During WWII, it was common for people to rent rooms by the week from homeowners. This provided all the necessities of having an apartment without the expense. If you moved here and wanted to work in the defense industry this would work until you could get your own apartment. Hartford had a nationally known actress named Marietta Canty. When I was growing up she lived in Hollywood. When she retired she resided on Mahl Avenue. One of the best afternoons I ever spent was at a wedding reception. Marietta Canty and I were table guests. She told me about the roles she used to play, as a maid and the people she knew. City Councilman Kyle Anderson is her great nephew. His grandparents owned the house on Mahl Avenue that is on the freedom trail. She had a brother named Arnold Canty who used to play guitar and sing. He played in New York for a while and the last time I heard him perform was in the late 1940's, between 1948 and 1950, at A. Rathskeller on Hillside Avenue. A. Rathskeller was a basement nightclub and we used to have them all over Hartford. They went by different names and the one where he played that night was called Cyprus Arms. We used to have a joke that went "when the depression hit, my old man didn't jump out of a window" and the reply would be "yeah that's because he was drunk in A. Rathskeller. He was already below ground, how's he going to jump out of a window when he has to jump up to reach the ground?"

In addition to all of this we had the 1st Company Governors Foot Guard Hall. We used to have bands, fight cards and wrestling matches. I use to go to the fights but I never went to wrestling. My gym teacher at Arsenal School (Smiler Livingston) used to be a referee for wrestling matches there. He used to tell me that at one time he was a wrestler himself. I remember seeing Charlie Barnett's band there too. Although she was not with him when I saw him, Lena Horne was on the road with him at one time. Also there was Buddy Johnson, Andy Kerk and his Clouds of Joy, Illinois Jack, and several other big bands. Later on, when I was grown, Tom Parish and Sonny Fredericks used to book acts there. I don't know when they stopped bringing acts there. I have asked myself several times when and why. The 1st Company Governors Foot Guard Hall was very important to us at one time because it was totally available to the black community. It's still standing, there on High Street.

We Move out of the Old Neighborhood

My Father bought the house at 676-678 Garden Street in 1949. That was 64 years ago. We moved the year after he bought it. I remember coming up here to shovel snow after he had bought the house. He must have bought it in the summer of 1949 and we moved in the spring of 1950. One of the benefits of moving into the new house included getting a telephone. It was our first one. About five years later we got our first television set. My father had a garden that went all the way to the back yards of Martin Street. He planted everything including two weeping willow trees. Although they provided quick shade they ate up your whole house including the foundation and your plumbing because the roots look for water. He also planted collard greens, cabbage, corn, carrots, everything. He had a peach tree and strawberries. The peaches grew so low that you could reach up and pick them. When my nephew, Reggie, was a little boy he used to say "my granddaddy say those are my strawberries, why are you always eating them?" Next door to the north our neighbors used to grow plums and pears.

Here's my father next to his garden behind the house at 676-678 Garden Street

Here's my mother at around the same time.

John F. Kennedy's visit to Main and Pavilion

I was there to see John F. Kennedy when he was running for the office of President of the United States. His car stopped at the intersection of Main, Mahl Avenue and Pavilion. He was on his way to the portico of the Times building where he spoke. The next month he was elected to office.

In addition to seeing John F. Kennedy in Hartford, I saw him at the Army/Navy game in 1962. Initially, he sat on the Army side. Then, at half time the mid-shipmen and cadets lined up at the fifty yard line and he walked across the football field so that he could sit on the Navy side. When he got about halfway across some guy broke in between two of the cadets and puts his hand up like he was a photographer taking a picture. Suddenly someone grabbed this guy and took him to where the President came from and brought him through a fence. We never saw him again. When the President got over to the Navy side, I was sitting around twenty or thirty yards away from where he was sitting. His face was flushed bloody red. That guy could have killed him if he wanted to. I saw film footage of this on television that night around five times and could never tell where the guy came from, or where they took him. As they escorted him off the field he was literally off the ground. They locked him up but they let him go in a couple of days because he was harmless, he wasn't trying to do anything, but he could have. The night the President was killed I remember thinking that I saw the preamble to his assassination. I'll never forget that even with the Army, Navy and the Secret Service there, that guy was close enough to get him. There were 103,000 people there but not a single ticket was sold at the game. They were all acquired through Congressional offices, Senatorial Offices or the Army/Navy Cadets. Before the game, all of the traffic flowed from downtown to the stadium and after the game; it flowed the other way. Parking was free.

Politics, Hartford Style

This town is a different breed of cat... William "Rab" Smith

The political tactics used nowadays is nothing new. Over fifty years ago, in 1962, when John Clark ran for City Council we had "palm cards". In those days every district there was someone popular. For example in the Charter Oak Avenue area there was a strong Polish presence and a guy named Polowski was running for council. He was very popular down there, so we had cards printed up "Polowski and Clark" When people in the Charter Oak Avenue area would see Polowski and Clark on the same card they would naturally assume that Clark was a running mate. That way you would steal a few votes where you couldn't win. If you did the same thing in areas where you could win you could put together a winner. Also, in those days you could call ahead to a place that provided rides to the opposition. Because the phones didn't hang up automatically in those days, you could leave the phone off the hook and no one at the other end could used that phone nor could anybody call them which is even more important. You could do that with all of the headquarters. A call in those days cost a nickel.

You would get a handful of nickels and tie up all the phones of the opposition.

Some of the work was not as devious. Tom Parish (owner of the gas station on the corner of Main and Pavilion) would go around with your uncle, Ben, with a loud speaker on the top of a truck, announcing who to vote for.

Here we all are; my sister Thelma, my brother Charlie, me, my sister Barbara, and my brother Ben.

Although it seems like we were all about the same age, we were kind of spread apart. To illustrate how true this is, as I went off to war, Barbara was just ten years old. At first we used to call her "Maxi Bear" after Max Bear the fighter, and then we used to call her "Mutt" because she was the littlest.

Here are the husband and wives of the Smith children, from left to right: Winick Drayton (Barbara's husband), my wife Agnes, my brother-in-law Tom (Thelma's husband), and my sister-in-law Eunice (Ben's wife). My brother, Charlie, married years after this photo was taken in 1973 to his wife, Frances.

Here's my mother and my sister, Thelma, in Keney Park.

How to Improve the Standing of Hartford's Black People

When I was a kid, selling newspapers, I periodically would wander into the Polish American Club on Charter Oak Avenue. If the Lithuanians had functions they would be on one side of the hall and the Polish people would be on the other side. However, when their children started marrying each other, they became one. That's the same thing with the Italians and the Irish. When Front Street began to close down, the Catholic Church attended by the Italians was merged with the Catholic Church attended by the Irish and they became Saint Patrick's and Saint Anthony's which is on Ann Ucello and Church Street. What I'm saying is that these groups were made to interact with one another and they formed alliances that exist even today.

A lot of the challenges we now face are over jobs. Citizens are mad at illegal immigrants because the citizens can't find work but the illegal aliens can find work. The reason the illegal aliens can find work is because its work that no citizens will take. As a child I remember peoples using the term "that's nigger work" which meant that it was work they would not take. Even during times of slavery the barbers, the masons and other tasks were performed by slaves. The moment slavery ended and those professions began to unionize and make more money, it was no longer "nigger work." Then the blacks were pushed out of these positions. It would be another one hundred years before blacks could join the unions. Right here in Hartford, I got out of the Hartford Trade School at 111 Washington Street, and could not get into the union because of segregation. Basically, it works like this; although the contractor pays the bills, the union has the jobs and they sublet the jobs to the contractors. For blacks, it's been tooth and nail. You couldn't go to a contractor's office to get work because all of the help came from the union hall. The contractors would tell you point blank "if you get into the union we will give you a job." You would go to the union hall and they would take your name but nothing ever happened. Some people decided to squawk about it and the unions said "we'll go to court before we let them in." Two people, Mansfield Tilley, who became my business partner in Tilley's electric and Warren Stewart, went to court. It was the first complaint brought to the Fair Employment Practice Commission by anyone in the United States of America that I know of. Boce Barlow (for whom the street "Boce Barlow Way" was named) was the lawyer for the case. The case was battled for five years and it went to the State Supreme court. The Union spent fifty thousand dollars defending itself, between 1948-1953. Fifty thousand dollars was real money in those days. But the union still lost. Tragically, after the court case was won in favor of Blacks joining the electrical union, an attempt was made to get Blacks in the plumbers union. The plumbers union was immediately receptive so we had about 8, inner city Black young men, apply. They were hired at a pay rate that was so much money that they didn't know how to handle it. For some of them it was the worst thing that could have happened to them because they spent the money on things that almost destroyed them.

We've come a long ways but only so far. From the time that we've been in this community until now we've lost a lot of ground. We've been up and down and flatlined. We don't have people to take our place. By the time some of us reach the top it's time for the others of our age to retire.

Words for future generations

The Madison was a dance that was 2 steps forward and 3 steps back. Just like our culture. Our society allowed drugs to enter our neighborhoods because they thought the only place it would be is in the Black community. When it started affecting other races, we began the "war on drugs." What we need is a war on where drugs come from. People in the ghetto don't have planes, trains, ships or any other means to get drugs here.

What did we have to overcome to get to where we are today? So much of our ancestor's time and energy was spent just surviving. If they had been Yale graduates there's a good chance that you are a Yale grad but if they worked night and day just to feed themselves where is the money going to come from to send anyone to school? If it is your child that you want to send to school, you might need them in the ditch with you or on the farm with you. You've got to survive before you can do anything else. It's all relevant.

It kills me to hear someone say that they did everything that was necessary for them to get ahead. Do you know the people who could hardly read or write and made it possible for you to get the job you have? The Masons, The Elks, The Odd Fellows, the Knights of Pythias, The NAACP and our churches. Those are the people that put it on the line for you. So who are you doing it for? Some people say "well I take care of my kids." That's not good enough!

In 1963 I attended a function where Netty Bates attended. She had the Little Rock 9 with her. The Elks were going to provide them with scholarships to go to college. We were there in 1963 because it was the 100th anniversary of the Emancipation Proclamation. I thought it was more important than going to Washington D.C., for the march. Since I could actually see the event I attended, it was more important to me. Although the march turned out to be the event that got the voting rights act of 1964 passed. All these things were made possible in part by the great organizations like the Elks and the Masons but we don't trumpet it.

They decimated the Black community businesswise and educationally when they started integration. All of the Black teachers in the south were automatically out of a job. They couldn't work anymore because they weren't allowed to work in an integrated school. They were told that they didn't have what it takes, that they couldn't pass the test. They also said the same thing about Black people voting. If you couldn't pass a test you could not vote. Some of the people who took those tests were school teachers, so some oddball question would be made up and asked of the person that no one could answer unless they were told the answer in advance. Questions like "who was the first mayor of this town?" No one needed to know that. They didn't want them to pass it, and if the registrar didn't want you to pass, you didn't pass. They even had a poll tax from time to time. Anybody that didn't have two dollars couldn't pass. In the 1930's they had poll taxes right here in Connecticut. My father didn't have to pay it because he was a veteran of WWI. I can remember this so it wasn't that long ago. I don't believe my Mother voted until they outlawed the poll tax. Women didn't have the right to vote at all until 1920. This is the greatest country in the world but we had a lot of bumps in the road. We have had two Black mayors, Thirman Milner and Carrie Saxon Perry but it was never reflected in the workforce. With two Hispanic mayors, Eddie Perez and Pedro Segarra, you can tell who's in charge by looking at who is riding around in City of Hartford vehicles. Our mayors were too busy being fair.

A Word to the Wise

You build over a century. This country was not run by people who came over on the Mayflower. What was on the Mayflower? Some of them were bonded servants, indentured servants and the dregs out of prisons. These were the people that were not wanted in England. The people on the Mayflower left England in search of religious freedom and some of them were some of the most bigoted people in the world, but they took care of themselves. Other people gained ground through that system by doing the things that they didn't want to do. First the Irish came over and they became Firemen and Cops. They needed big guys to keep the order for them. Sooner or later these men sent their kids to school and those kids became in charge of things. And what did they do? Many of them did the same thing as some of the people who came over on the Mayflower.

Everybody understands it if you take care of your own. I didn't invent nepotism. Who better to watch your back than your brother? You've got to put your foot in the door before you can get inside of the room, and once you get in there don't let anybody put you out. Play the game for all it's worth because it's the only game in town. It's like a woman talking to a gambler when she says "why do you keep going over there don't you know that that game is crooked?" And the gambler says "yes but it's the only game in town so I'm going over there and play it every day." If you quit playing, you are out of the game.

This photograph appeared in the newspaper. The wording in the article was as follows:

William R. Smith was honored at a testimonial dinner on Sunday May 21, 1978 at Charter Oak Lodge No. 67, 650 Blue Hills Avenue, Hartford, Connecticut. Mr. Smith was singled out for his long years of service in Elkdom, civic and political affairs. Mr. Smith served as District Deputy of the Northern District for 14 years. Prior to that, Smith was 1st Vice President of the New England States and Eastern Canada, Assoc. of Elks. Mr. Smith is District Aide to Congressman William R. Cotter and also a member of the Hartford Democratic Town

Committee. Judge William D. Graham of the Court of Common Pleas was the principle speaker. (Left to right) Judge Graham, Charity Ann Jones, Mr. and Mrs. William R. Smith.

Exalted Ruler William "Rab" Smith at the Canton Street Elks Club October 1958

I Remember Hartford

The End

AN OPEN LETTER TO MY DAD:

Growing up on Garden Street all my friends had both parents. It was great how every parent looked out for all the children on the street.

I remember as a child in fifth grade at Brackett-Northeast my Caucasian teacher asked the class to do an essay on their hero. Most of the children wrote about President Kennedy, a baseball player or a basketball player who were all white. I wrote about you. We all had to stand up in class and read our essay. You know how I hated that although you always taught me to stand tall, and to speak plain and clear so that I can be heard. Before I could finish reading my teacher took me outside the room and asked me to change my hero to maybe someone I see on television (which at that time was all white people). I told her no. The next day at school, all of the essays were on the wall except mine. Everyone got an A+, A, B+. I got a C. I asked my teacher for my essay to bring home. I was so proud of my essay because it was about you, Dad. I brought that essay home and read it to you and Mom which made you two very happy. You know Mom. Besides saying I deserved an A she said some things I can't repeat here. You know what I mean.

As I expanded my horizons as a teenager I found out that some of my teen friends were not as fortunate as me. They didn't have a father. That is when I discovered Mother's day and not the one in May. One of my friends told me that she used to run over our house every morning to say prayers with us. She is a dentist now. That shows that prayers do work. Another friend said that she loved coming to our house at dinner time because we all sat down as a family and that I had a father that ate with us. She is a manager at a department store. Boy do I remember those days when it was our turn to discuss what went on during our day. You and Mom never got to say how your day went due to the fact that my siblings and I monopolized all of the time. Now that I have grown up, I remember that you did something that most people don't do. You listened to us.

Dad, I am so proud of you. You never cursed, spanked or called us out of the name you gave us. You made sure that we were a tight family. We always had food on our plates, a roof over our heads and you didn't mind if sometimes there was an extra plate on the table. Sometimes I look back at the past and see how selfish I was but you were always letting me make my mistakes and helping me to pick up the pieces without condemning me. Dad, your guidance helped me be the strong, black woman that I am today. Dad, I wouldn't trade you in for a Gucci bag and you know I love Gucci.

Dad, all those years ago you were my hero and you are still my hero. I wish all the children of today could experience what it is to have a dad, granddad, great-granddad, and a great-great-granddad like you.

Thank you Dad for being my hero

Love always,
Sharon Smith, Daughter

Dad,

"Like father, like son"; "a chip off the old block" and "the apple doesn't fall far from the tree" – are all terms we've heard that mean a son will have traits similar to his father upon reaching adulthood.

Some say I look like you, speak like you and act like you. As a young boy, I didn't see this and couldn't imagine it either. However, as I now reflect back over the years, I remember many things of my past.

First, your presence always commanded attention. Sharply dressed and impeccably polished, everyone noticed you. They also paid very careful attention to who you were, where you'd been and where you were going. And we all wanted to follow in your footsteps and travel the paths you'd chosen.

Second, I remember the way you always spoke and spoke up. Your words were always eloquent and carefully chosen. But most importantly, I remember that you spoke the truth – no matter how painful or unpleasant it may have made others feel. I know today that those impacted by your words and truthfulness, we are better people today.

Third, I remember that whatever you decided to do, you did it right; with style and you did it the best way that you could. From raising, teaching and mentoring me to taking care of our family, being a great father, husband and friend to many including some of my friends.

Now that I'm a grown man and have had many chances to reflect on my past, not only do I understand why some said what they said and I see it now. I am the man that I am today, because of you Dad. Thank you for the traits and for being you – the way you look, the way you speak and the way you act! I love you Dad.

Your son,

Billy

Dear Daddy,

As I sit here reflecting back on my life you are and were a hands on Dad. I remember asking you "have you ever seen God?" The explanation you gave me is the same one that I gave my son. I remember us riding all over Connecticut looking for shoes for me because I didn't want Spauldings.

I remember the trip to New York when they were building the World's Fair and you telling us when they finish building it, you were going to take us, and you did. I remember you teaching me how to write a check and wanting to teach me about how to read stocks. I wasn't interested but now I wish I had listened. But most of all I remember the love, patience, and guidance. Thank you. You are the best Dad. I am so proud to be your daughter. As you remember Hartford, I remember you. A great and wonderful Dad.

Love,

Deane

Made in the USA
Columbia, SC
09 October 2020